GOVERNMENT, ETHICS, AND MANAGERS

Government, Ethics, and Managers

A GUIDE TO SOLVING ETHICAL DILEMMAS IN THE PUBLIC SECTOR

Sheldon S. Steinberg
and
David T. Austern

PRAEGER

New York
Westport, Connecticut
London

Library of Congress Cataloging-in-Publication Data

Steinberg, Sheldon S.
Government, ethics, and managers : a guide to solving ethical
dilemmas in the public sector / Sheldon S. Steinberg and David T.
Austern.
p. cm.
Includes bibliographical references.
ISBN 0–275–93637–6 (alk. paper)
1. Corruption (in politics)—United States. 2. Political ethics—
United States. I. Austern, David. II. Title.
JK2249.S76 1990
320.973—dc20 90–7146

British Library Cataloguing in Publication Data is available.

A hardcover edition of *Government, Ethics, and Managers* is available from
the Quorum Books imprint of Greenwood Publishing Group, Inc. (ISBN
0–89930–442–7).

Library of Congress Catalog Card Number: 90–7146
ISBN: 0–275–93637–6

First published in 1990

Praeger Publishers, One Madison Avenue, New York, NY 10010
An imprint of Greenwood Publishing Group, Inc.

Printed in the United States of America

The paper used in this book complies with the
Permanent Paper Standard issued by the National
Information Standards Organization (Z39.48–1984).

10 9 8 7 6 5 4 3 2 1

To Stella and Marilyn, our ethical role models

Contents

Preface

Unethical practices in the public sector have been with us since the first colonists arrived in America. Since then, no period in U.S. history has been without its own kind of fraud, waste, and abuse by the public officials appointed by the Crown, by the political party in power, or by the acts and misdeeds of elected or career public servants. It's as if the American symbols of mom and apple pie share center stage with unethical practices.

Changing times bring changes in unethical practices and, to some extent, a change in their focus. Although common threads such as political spoils, political influence, and insider information about procurements continue to poison the practice of government, changes in public perception about politicians of any persuasion have led to a narrowing of the opportunities and incentives for unethical practices. The problem of unethical practices in the public sector persists, however, and will continue as long as government leaders continue to tolerate and, even worse, contribute to the problem.

The fact that government leaders continue to contribute to the problem is the primary motivation for this book. There's a lot of funny stuff going on out there, and it's been going on for a long time. In fact, the genesis of this book was a series of regional training workshops on maintaining municipal integrity in which we were involved more than a decade ago. The series, sponsored by the National Institute of Law Enforcement and Criminal Justice, Law Enforcement Assistance Administration, was presented across the country to some 1,000 police chiefs, district attorneys, city managers, county executives, and other public policy executives and decisionmakers. The basic ethical concepts and management practices reviewed and discussed in the workshop series have been expanded upon and included here to reflect current ethical dilemmas facing the people who work for us and are paid by tax dollars. We acknowledge that the vast majority are honest and earn their salaries. We also acknowledge that there's still a lot of funny stuff going on that can be detected and prevented a lot earlier than it is. We further acknowledge that there are in place many laws, administrative procedures, and other checks and balances that, if followed and applied regularly, could prevent most unethical practices.

We believe that government executives and managers carry the primary responsibility for leadership in developing and maintaining an ethical climate of government practice. That they have failed is evident from opinion-poll results during the past two decades. Elected, appointed, and career public officials are not viewed as ethical people. As a result, a major threat to our political system is the continuing disenchantment of our electorate, and the resolution of the problem lies with the public officials.

Government, Ethics, and Managers: A Guide to Solving Ethical Dilemmas in the Public Sector, deals with dilemmas faced by public officials and explores the reasons for their unethical behavior. It looks at the costs of unethical practices and profiles three kinds of government practitioners—the Corrupter, the Functionary, and the Ethicist. These sections are aimed at setting the stage for reader introspection and the ethical climate of the reader's community. In the last two chapters we look at and detail the management of the ethical practice of government through training, investigation, and management control.

We wish to acknowledge the many city, county, state, and federal managers and executives who participated in the local and regional workshops and the national conferences of the National League of Cities and International Association of City Managers for helping shape much of our thinking on this subject. In particular, we wish to thank the members of the Maintaining Municipal Integrity Workshop team: Chief John H. Ball, Chief Victor I. Cizanckas, Thomas W. Fletcher, Theodore R. Lyman, and Ora A. Spaid; and our colleagues at the National Institute for Law Enforcement and Criminal Justice: Paul J. Cascarano, Louis A. Mayo, G. Martin Lively, and John W. Bonner.

Finally, we want to thank Faye Haskins, who diligently and uncomplainingly typed many drafts of this book.

1

Dilemmas of the Ethical Practice of Government

ARE YOU OR WOULD YOU BE AN ETHICAL PUBLIC EMPLOYEE?

The decade of the 1980s has seen a dramatic increase in unethical behavior by government employees at all levels. From the inner circle of the White House to local elected and appointed officials, scandal after scandal has been followed by indictments and convictions detailed in banner headlines in newspapers and reported on the evening electronic media. The 1990s will almost certainly witness the unethical fallout of its predecessor decade.

One could paraphrase Professor Harold Hill's warning in the Broadway musical and movie *The Music Man*, "We've Got Trouble in River City!" as "We've Got Trouble in You Name It." Not only do we have trouble in our nation's capitol, but we also have trouble in New York City, Montpelier, Chicago, Miami, Dallas, San Diego, and most points in between. This trouble exists in the legislative, executive, and judicial branches of government and at the local, county, state, and federal levels. Hill could point to officials for whom you voted and to officials appointed as part of your elected officials' patronage system. He could describe the trouble as fraud, waste, and abuse not only of government funds but of the public trust. The trouble is compounded by the erosion of the ethical basis and practice of government. This leads to the public believing that "All politicians are the same; my vote doesn't really matter."

The range of unethical and corrupt practices covers almost every aspect of the practice of government. This involves insider information on zoning and land use and improperly accepting gifts for political favors. It includes failure to disclose conflicts of interest whereby an elected or appointed official receives monetary gain as a result of an unethical vote or influence in the legislative context. Corrupt practices have the effect of poisoning the well of the public trust and confidence in our democratic form of government. They erode the participation of our fellow citizens and limit the broadest possible base for deciding who will represent us in local, county, state, and national governments. Such practices cause our brightest and best to seek careers outside of government.

Corrupt practices affect the work of government managers, supervisors, and their staffs. These tax-supported employees are charged with the day-to-day responsibility for collecting garbage, enforcing the law, paving and maintaining the streets, regulating utilities, protecting the environment, zoning for land use, and the myriad of other visible and behind-the-scenes services for which we pay. Corrupt practices can be found in all three branches of government. We wish it were not so, but as we will detail, all three branches have problems with the ethical practice of government.

The scope of the problem is difficult to quantify. The numbers involved give us some indication that the problem is both large and pervasive. Consider these facts: there are more than 82,000 local governments in the United States—county, municipal, township, school district, and special district. In addition, there are 50 state governments and the United States government with its millions of employees. Given the almost daily disclosures of unethical and illegal practices, indictments, and convictions of public employees who work at all levels of government in many jurisdictions, it is astonishing that the public is not more incensed than it is at the problem of corrupt practices in the government.

That the services we pay for are accomplished at all is not the ethical issue. The ethical issue is the cost and quality of these services and for how much less and at what higher quality they could be accomplished in a more ethical environment. The scandals at the Department of Housing and Urban Development (HUD) disclosed during 1989 have cost taxpayers billions of dollars. The savings and loan debacle and bailout will cost taxpayers an estimated $200 billion. The series of Defense Department scandals disclosed during each year of the last half of the 1980s not only inflated costs for defense systems and equipment but also resulted in the increased costs for weapons that did not work under battlefield conditions.

Corrupt practices, sadly, also involve accepted and legally sanctioned practices that contribute to the public's distrust of their elected representatives. As long as politicians can accept large honoraria and political contributions from special interests—individuals, corporations, associations, and political action committees—who can believe that the politicians will not be influenced in favor of the contributors? Indeed, the savings and loan scandal included the activities of United States senators who attempted to curtail a federal investigation into the loan procedures (later shown to be illegal) of a banking official who had contributed heavily to the political campaign of each senator.

A standard, predictable defense used by public officials at the first hint of an accusation of unethical practice is to blame the media. The media, however, did not cause Watergate, or Contragate, or Irangate. The media did not cause the parking scandal in New York City or the convictions of the vice-president of the United States, cabinet members, and department heads in Washington, D.C. The media did not cause the indictment and conviction of virtually scores of elected county board members and commissioners in Oklahoma. The media did not cause the laundry list of former President Reagan's indicted and convicted appointees.

The effect of the media on inquiries and reports of fraud, waste, and abuse is to cause the circling of government wagons for a last-ditch stand. A variety of stalling and delaying tactics are frequently employed to avoid documentation of the unethical act. The legislative history of the Freedom of Information Act reveals that one purpose of the act was to force government officials to release information that rightfully should have been available to the public. Sooner or later, however, the truth is revealed as it was recently in a medium-sized city in the Midwest.

In this city, the chief of police was removed from office for a variety of unethical and illegal acts. While the former chief was waiting for the expected grand jury indictment, a new chief of police was recruited and appointed. Shortly after his appointment, the new chief became curious about what had led his predecessor to stray ethically. He contacted the former chief and asked him what had happened. The former chief said he could not discuss the case but that he had left three envelopes in the lower left-hand desk drawer that would solve all the problems the new chief might have during the first three ethical situations he faced. The former chief cautioned his successor not to open the envelopes all at once but only in sequence.

The new chief was puzzled but, after checking to be sure the numbered envelopes were in the drawer, forgot about them and focused on his job. About a month later, the local press contained a story about unethical purchasing in the police department. The press clamored for a statement by the new chief. Not quite sure how to handle this but remembering the envelopes, the new chief took out envelope number one and opened it. It read, "Blame the problem on your predecessor." The new chief called a press conference and proceeded to do just that, explaining that he was only on the job a few weeks and had not had sufficient time to implement his own management controls. The press was satisfied, and the story died.

A month later another story appeared in the media concerning narcotics protection money. The chief returned to the drawer with the envelopes, opened the second envelope and read, "Tell them you are reorganizing, and you need more time before the effects will be apparent." The press conference the chief called in which he announced this explanation produced the same result as the previous press conference.

Two months later, a story broke about widespread payoffs to traffic police officers to stop them from issuing tickets for speeding and other traffic violations. This time it was clear that the new chief either knew or should have known about the payoffs.

The chief retreated to the drawer, opened the third envelope, and read, "Prepare three envelopes."

Circling the wagons also protects the unethical from the ethical, insiders who blow the whistle when they witness unethical practices. These "whistleblowers" who identify fraud, waste, and abuse in government practice are frequently viewed not as ethical role models to emulate but as the enemy. As noted later in this book, the chilling effect of sanctions imposed on whistleblowers further erodes the ethical practice of government. After a few instances in which whistleblowing behavior is punished, the message to others who have cause to blow the whistle is clear: "Why bother? Not only will nothing happen to remedy the situation, but something negative will happen to me."

There is no excuse for unethical behavior in the practice of government. Fraud, waste, and abuse have no place in government, and their costs in reduced or poor quality services requires that we refuse to accept unethical conduct on the part of government officials at all levels. The cost in erosion of confidence in our democratic way of life requires that each of us demand ethical conduct on the part of our elected and appointed officials.

Every day public employees face situations in which their personal and professional integrity and ethics are tested. For a number of years, therefore, during workshops around the country, we asked public officials to respond to and discuss the 14 "ethical dilemmas" presented below. More than 1,000 mayors, city managers, county executives, and other key local public officials answered, discussed, and debated these dilemmas. Now it is your turn.

ETHICAL DILEMMA QUESTIONS

The 14 ethical dilemmas all can be answered either yes or no. Read each dilemma and answer all 14. Check your answer with the answers that begin on page 12.

Although the answers also contain some analysis, this is a "forced-response" series on questions; that is, "maybe" and "it depends" are not acceptable answers.

In addition, although some questions may appear to have a

more obvious yes or no answer than other questions, we are prepared to argue that the response we have given is the only appropriate response to the dilemmas posed.

Finally, for each dilemma, assume you are the person who has to make the decision to resolve the dilemma, that is, the city manager, police chief, department head, and so on.

Question 1

You are the city manager or county executive of your county. The Board of Directors of the Chamber of Commerce has an annual weekend outing at a resort some miles from your city. During the weekend there is golf, tennis, swimming, card games, dinner dances with entertainment, and numerous cocktail parties. During the day there are sessions at which the chamber board reviews progress for the past year and discusses plans for the coming year. For several years, the city has contributed $100,000 annually for the support of the chamber.

You are invited to the chamber's weekend outing with all expenses paid by the chamber. *Do you accept the invitation and go for the weekend?*

Question 2

For many years, you and Frank Jordan have been close friends. You attended high school together and were college classmates. You were best man at each other's weddings. Your wives are good friends. For the past ten years, Frank and his wife have taken you and your wife to dinner on your birthday. It is just something he insists upon doing, and it has become a tradition. He can well afford it; Frank owns the largest plumbing supply business in the state and does more than $10 million in business each year with the unit of local government where you live.

You have been an insurance broker all your professional life. Three years ago you ran for a seat on the City Council and were elected. You maintain an active interest in your insurance business. You have just been named chairman of the council committee that oversees procurement contracts, including plumbing supplies.

Your birthday is coming up in a couple of weeks. Frank has called you to remind you that he and Mrs. Jordan have a special treat for your birthday dinner this year. He has made reservations at a fancy new restaurant that everyone is talking about. *Do you accept?*

Question 3

For ten years you have held a management position with your county government. You have enjoyed great success in this career, and you have risen to the post of county executive. Your spouse has told you that he or she wants to run for a post on the County Council, the elected body to which the county executive reports. *If your spouse is elected, can you continue to serve as county executive?*

Question 4

Assume you are the elected mayor of your community. A new Civic Plaza, which is in the planning stage, will restore the downtown area of your city. Because of inflation, the bond issue for development that was passed three years ago is already too little to insure completion of the project. A developer who wants to erect a high-rise office building and mall near the Civic Plaza offers to buy a large tract of undeveloped land in the plaza area and donate it to the city in exchange for permission to build his proposed building higher than the present zoning restrictions will permit.

He has made this offer to you and has left it up to you to decide whether to communicate the offer to the City Council. *Do you pass on the offer to the council?*

Question 5

George Stevens is a county clerk of your country; he reports to you with respect to his responsibilities and performance, and you have the authority to fire him. As part of his duties, George reviews all fines collected by the Traffic Court and checks them for both receipt of correct amounts and statutory authority for the fine levied. With respect to this responsibility and all others, George is sensationally good. He has an attention to detail that is nothing short of remarkable, and he performs his work in a timely fashion. In addition, George has a pleasing personality.

There is a story circulating about town; it concerns the arrest of a prominent county citizen who was stopped by the local police, scored a high 0.30 on a breathalizer test (0.10 is presumption of intoxication), and was found to be accompanied by Miss Jones, who boldly introduced herself to the police as a prostitute from Chicago. According to police records, her employment description is accurate. The story of this arrest was told at a local Elks meeting and is the favorite topic of conversation throughout the county. The prominent citizen has complained to you about this story, and your investigation has convinced you that George Stevens told the story at the Elks meeting. Despite the confidential nature of police reports, when you confront George with the facts, he admits he told the story. *Will you fire George?*

Question 6

Oscar Phillips has worked for the County Police Department for 19 years, steadily rising through the ranks to his present position of captain. Last week Phillips was called to the scene of an arrest made by two officers under his command. The person under arrest was Jordan, the son of Ford Hanks, president of the County Council. Ford Hanks was on the scene. Hanks claimed his son was innocent and had been framed by the police. The officers told Captain Phillips they had observed Jordan Hanks exceeding the speed limit by 25 miles per hours, had ordered him to pull over, and then had discovered in the back of the pickup truck Hanks was driving approximately 200 pounds of marijuana with a "street" value of $40,000. Jordan Hanks said he did not know how the marijuana came to be in the back of the truck, and Ford Hanks threatened both Captain Phillips and the arresting officers with loss of job, loss of pay, demotion of rank, and a suit for false arrest in the event his son was charged.

Apparently fearful for his job, Captain Phillips ordered the officers to let Jordan Hanks go, ordered them to destroy any written notes concerning the incident, took custody of the marijuana, and burned it.

The matter has been referred to you. *Will you fire Captain Phillips?*

Question 7

Your favorite brand of Scotch is Chevas Regal, but you don't buy it too often because it is so expensive. You have told this to the liquor dealer from whom you buy your booze. It's a kind of joke. "Think rich and drink cheap," you sometimes remark when you buy a less expensive brand.

The liquor dealer gets in trouble for taking bets on horses, and his license is in jeopardy. Although you are a middle management public official in your community, you have nothing to do with the hearing on suspension of the license. The next time you buy liquor, however, you discover when you get home that the bag containing your liquor includes a fifth of the Chevas Regal, which you neither ordered nor paid for. *Do you return the Scotch?*

Question 8

A physician friend of yours asks if you would be interested in investing in a doctors' building that a group of physicians are planning to erect in the city of which you are manager. No decisions involving your job are expected as part of the investment; the doctors are simply selling shares in their venture. It will be next to a shopping center in a rapidly growing part of town.

You stand to more than quadruple the $24,000 cost of a share in a short time, and maybe make even more than that. You have the money. *Would you invest in the doctors' building?*

Question 9

The county is in need of 20 new vehicles, 15 to be used by the police department and 5 to be used for general services.

State and county practice requires purchase from the lowest bidder. The County Council has determined that Ford sedans should be purchased. A local car dealer has offered to supply all 20 cars for a total price of $220,000, but a dealer in a county 30 miles away has offered comparably equipped cars for $200,000. *Can you purchase the cars from the local dealer at the higher price?*

Question 10

Hazel Stevens is a valued employee. She has worked for you for years, and she is the kind of worker you can depend on to put in extra time and effort when it is needed. She is always there in a crisis, and several times she has handled situations that would have been uncomfortable for you. You really owe her a lot.

Recently, Hazel came to you and admitted that for some time she has been "borrowing" money from the petty cash fund and writing false receipts to cover it. It was never much, usually $10 or $15, and she always repaid it. But her conscience has bothered her so much that she had to confess.

Under your personnel policies, her action is clearly a cause for dismissal. *Do you fire her?*

Question 11

During the six-year period you worked in your city's government, you supervised a number of multimillion dollar contracts. You received an offer to join a private firm that looked too good to refuse, and you left your city job. Unfortunately, the job didn't work out because of poor financial management over which you had no control. You spent about five months seeking a full-time job. During this period you were asked to come back as a consultant to the company you left to help the new owners try to get the company back on its feet. You worked for them a total of six days. Unexpectedly, your old job in the city government opened up. You applied and were hired after going through the required competitive process.

About a year later, your agency announced a procurement

very similar to those you previously monitored. Your supervisor asked you to serve on the Source Selection Board. You accepted. Shortly after that, one of the new owners of your old consulting firm called to see how you were doing. In the course of the conversation, he asked about the procurement, saying he was thinking of putting in a bid. You told him you could not discuss it, and he did not pursue the matter further. *Do you resign as chair of the Source Selection Board?*

Question 12

You have been asked to speak at a Sunday brunch meeting of the Board of Alderman of a small city across the river, which is the state line, from the city of which you are the city manager. The Board of Alderman has asked you to tell it about your budget reduction program in anticipation of a Proposition 13 type of measure that is pending before its state legislature.

At the conclusion of your speech, the chair of the meeting hands you an envelope containing an honorarium check for $250 and explains, "This is in appreciation of your giving up your Sunday morning." *Do you accept the honorarium?*

Question 13

For some time, police officers on two adjacent beats have met each day for a coffee break at a restaurant near a place where the three beats intersect. They usually have coffee and danish and occasionally a piece of pie.

You are newly assigned to one of the beats. When you go for the coffee break for the first day and you walk to the cashier to pay the check, and proprietor says, "No charge. I am glad to have you officers around." The other officers leave without paying. *Do you pay your check?*

Question 14

Henry Settles is a person who has worked in your department for a long time. He is conscientious, maybe too conscientious, at least in the view of many of his fellow workers. He is always at work on time, always puts in all hours expected, and works very hard. But he expects everyone else to do the same, and he frequently complains about other employees who are tardy or who take long lunch hours or who call in sick when almost everyone knows they are not sick.

Recently, Henry reported to you that some employees were making unauthorized copies on the department's copier. Worse, in Henry's view, they were using their department telephone to make local, personal calls during the workday. You issued a memorandum concerning these practices, but since then Henry has been *persona non grata* with many of his fellow employees. Henry is a probable candidate for a new position, one that would mean a promotion for him. *Do you promote Henry?*

ETHICAL DILEMMA ANSWERS

Many years ago, Supreme Court Justice Felix Frankfurther commented that "in law also the right answer usually depends on putting the right question" (*Rogers v. Commissioner*, 320 U.S. 410, 413 [1943]). In the same vein, the Greek philosopher Solan observed that we should never confuse the ability to ask difficult questions with the ability to answer them. Solan lived what he preached. He wrote the Greek constitution; then he promptly packed his bags and left the country so that, as he announced, nobody would be able to ask him what the various parts of the constitution meant. Alas, we are unable to do that, tempting though it may be, because it would be unfair—perhaps even unethical.

It is more fun to ask questions than to answer them. That is particularly true of the questions we have asked. With few exceptions, reasonable people might disagree with respect to the most appropriate answer to each of the questions asked. Then, too, some of the questions have no answers, at least not to the extent an "answer" provides cloture to a question. Rather, many of the questions raise other questions and evoke comment as a substitute for solution.

What follows are our best thoughts with respect to what has been asked. You should know that a significant part of these answers is not a product of our intellect. As noted above, we have asked these same questions to over more than 1,000 government officials. We have listened to their responses and heard them grapple with these ethical dilemmas. We have discovered that if you become a discussion leader, you inevitably learn from the participants. We have learned from all of them, and we are grateful for that experience.

Answer to Question 1

Do you accept the invitation to the chamber of commerce weekend? A lot can be said for attending the weekend as a guest of the chamber. With decreasing economic clustering and a shrinking overall tax base in many communities, chambers are important for the financial health and development of every unit of local government. In addition, the weekend is not totally devoted to fun and games; progress and plans will be discussed. Finally, at least some thought has been given to the chamber's importance to the community; a not insignificant sum of money is contributed to the chamber by the local government each year. It is important for local government officials to be knowledgeable about what the chamber plans to do; by attending the meeting, a local official can participate in and perhaps influence such plans.

The appearance of such attendance is bad, however, and we believe the bad appearance, at least in this case, outweighs the potential good. Describe it in any terms you want, but the fact remains that you, as a local official, are attending a resort meeting—free rooms, cocktails, food, golf fees, and so on—while you hold an elected or appointed office that permits you to assist the chamber in many of its activities. In addition, the unit of government you represent almost certainly does business with chamber officials, officers, or members. There is nothing inherently wrong with that, but your independence as a public official appears to be at least partially compromised by accepting the free weekend from the chamber. Integrity in public office is not easy to define. But we believe it is threatened when a public official accepts gratuities in the amount described in this question.

In addition, we cannot help but speculate that, depending on the sensitivity of the chamber members in attendance, the city manager or county executive may be asked for favors—removal of parking restrictions in front of certain business establishments, a moratorium on the collection of sales taxes, a change in certain zoning rules—all within and without his or her power to grant.

Although a yes or no choice does not permit a middle ground, there may be a compromise position. Why not attend—but pay your own way—and make it clear in advance that such financial arrangement is a condition precedent to your attendance.

Answer to Question 2

Do you accept the invitation to the new restaurant? Sad though it may be, we believe one of the strongest arguments in favor of not going to dinner with Jordan is to ask yourself the following question: What would you believe if you read in the local newspaper that an elected official had been seen at dinner with Jordan under the circumstances described in this question?

Upon assuming office, however, elected or appointed public officials do not have to give up all friendships and prior associations. Public employment requires many sacrifices, but it should not require that. Inevitably, some people who do not know of your long friendship but are aware of your City Council position and Frank Jordan's business, will assume the worst if they see you at dinner. Again, that is unfortunate but, we believe, tolerable under the circumstances.

We assume, in addition, that you will abstain from both vote and comment with respect to Jordan's business if the subject appears on the City Council agenda.

Some people have suggested that it would be more appropriate to go to Jordan's home for the celebration. Perhaps, but is it not true that by meeting in a public place you dispel suspicion? (We warned you that some questions must raise other questions.) Finally, although it lacks charm, grace, and a host of other qualities, it might be appropriate for you to split the check with Jordan—and make a show of it for the benefit of the suspicious eyes observing you.

Answer to Question 3

Can you remain in office as county executive? This is a growing problem in many professions, particularly as more and more women are elected or appointed to public office and accepted more willingly in the professions. Kathryn Hepburn and Spencer Tracy presented the first example of a similar problem in a well-known motion picture—he playing the role of a prosecutor and she appearing as a defense attorney. Presently, the husband of a Supreme Court justice practices law in Washington, D.C., and the husband of a civil agency head practices law in a partnership that represents institutions over which his wife has some jurisdiction.

We do not believe it is appropriate to limit public service to one member of a family. The American Bar Association has held that two members of a family—including husband and wife, under certain circumstances—can represent opposing interests in litigation. The reason given for this ruling is that the practice of law should not be limited one to a family. We believe the same rule is appropriate for public employment. In this question, though, if the spouse of the county executive is elected to the County Council, such spouse may not vote or discuss—or in our view, be present—when the employment of the county executive appears on the agenda of the County Council.

This is a good point to raise another question—the answer to which is converse to the answer to this question. It sometimes happens that practicing attorneys serve on elected boards or commissions at the local level. To what extent should a member of a County Council who is an attorney be permitted to represent clients against the county? Most courts that have addressed this particular conflict of interest have held that an attorney is prohibited from representing a client against the unit of local government that he or she has been elected to represent. See *Higgins v. Advisory Committee on Professional Responsibility*, 373 A.2d 372 (1977); *People v. Municipal Court*, 138 Cal. Rptr. 235 (1977); and *Georgia Department of Human Resources v. Sistruck*, 291 S.E.2d 524 (1982). One court reached an opposite result: *City of Hoquiam v. Public Employment Relations Commission*, 646 P.2d 129 (1982).

Answer to Question 4

Do you pass the offer on to the council? There are some arguments that can be advanced for rejecting the "donation" of the undeveloped land without bringing the offer to the attention of the City Council. This "gift" is obviously in exchange for a zoning variance. The appearances of this gift are unfortunate, and changes in zoning laws frequently lead to someone's economic advantage and a decrease in another person's property value.

On the other hand, we view this as a separation-of-powers issue, and to state it directly, we believe it is wholly inappropriate for a city manager or country executive to withhold information from a decision-making authority. Indeed, we cannot even conceptualize a situation in which the executive or manager should act as a filter of ethical problems.

Answer to Question 5

Will you fire George for gossiping about the confidential report? In almost every jurisdiction, under some circumstances, a government employee may be fired for revealing confidential information. Such a rule, however, frequently requires that the revelation of the confidential information be for the purpose of economic gain. It is important to remember that the noneconomic gain revelation frequently causes just as much harm as the revelation that is more typically corrupt.

Public employees cannot be reminded too frequently that confidential information is just that, confidential. The more interesting the information, the more juicy the scandal, and the more likely we are all tempted to disclose it—to our friends, to our fellow employees, to our colleagues at a social gathering. We all believe we can disguise the identity of someone likely to be embarrassed so that no harm will come to such person. But it never turns out that way.

Would we fire George? Under the facts described, no. But we would suspend him and reprimand him. Also, we would use this event as a reminder to all employees that public employment means public confidence and trust—and that confidential information is to be kept secret except when there is specific authorization to disclose.

Answer to Question 6

Will you fire Captain Phillips for burning the marijuana and destroying the notes? A colleague of ours, a former city manager, tells the story of the four men in the sanitation crew who kept the scrap metal they accumulated in the course of their official duties (instead of turning it over to the city) and every month sold it to a scrap metal dealer. The city also sold scrap metal. One of the four men was the supervisor/foreman; he never shared in the proceeds of the illicit sales, but he knew about the practice, and once a month he drove the truck to the scrap metal dealer, where the other three men sold the scrap and pocketed the proceeds. When the scheme was discovered, the personnel director recommended to our friend the city manager that the three workers be fired and the foreman be suspended without pay for 60 days. The city manager reversed this recommendation; he fired the foreman and suspended the workers for 60 days.

We believe the city manager was right, and for the same reason we would fire Captain Phillips. Supervision or a command position means just that—you are not one of the gang, you do not "go along" with everyone else, and you should not be subject to intimidation. Supervisors are paid more for greater responsibility, and they should be prepared to exercise it. We realize the result seems harsh—and it is—but nobody drafted Captain Phillips to be a police officer, and nobody forced him to assume the rank of captain.

Two further considerations: First, if it seems to you that the personnel discipline in Answer 5 is significantly less severe than the personnel discipline in Answer 6, we acknowledge that it is, but we believe that interference with the administration of justice is a greater threat to the integrity of public employment than a breach of confidentiality. Second, we would use the dismissal of Captain Phillips as an occasion to seek the reinstatement of charges against Jordan Hanks and the prosecution of his father for obstruction of justice.

Unfair question time: What sanction, if any, would you impose on the two police officers who obeyed Captain Phillips's clearly illegal order?

Answer to Question 7

Do you return the scotch? We do not believe it is appropriate to forbid all public employees from accepting any gift of any kind for any reason. Such a rule, while easy to enforce, can lead to absurd results: what about birthday or wedding presents from long-time acquaintances or relatives? On the other hand, the acceptance of gratuities can raise questions of integrity.

We believe there are some reasonable rules to apply to the questions of gifts. First, gifts from relatives should be permitted. Second, on special occasions, that is, birthdays, weddings, and so on, gifts from close friends should also be permitted provided that such gifts are of some minimum value, for instance, $25 or less. Third, and most important, the recipient must look to the purpose of the gift: Is it a gift, or is it an attempt to influence the official? In reaching a decision as to purpose, the recipient should consider not only the relationship of the giver but the previous history—if any—of the exchange or giving of presents. When in doubt, the gift should be refused. All gifts, of any kind, should be reported to a supervisor or other appropriate official. Based on the foregoing, you return the Scotch—at once.

Answer to Question 8

Will you invest in the doctors' building? This is a close question. Generally, federal law does not prohibit federal officials from investing unless the investment presents a direct or potential conflict with their official duties. If that standard were applied to these facts, the investment probably would be permitted because "no decisions involving your job are expected." In addition, public service should not be a barrier to investing in profitable ventures.

The prudent person, however, might ask why the physician friend brought this venture to your attention in the first place. Will the Buildings Department and other inspection or enforcement agencies know of your investment? Will that influence their employees in any way? If so, does that answer the ultimate question?

Under the circumstances, assuming that seeking an advantage is not the purpose of the offer to invest, we believe you can invest in the building. You must be careful to make sure your investment—and the identity of you as an investor—is not used in an improper way by your coinvestors.

Answer to Question 9

Can you purchase the cars from the local dealer? We believe that you must follow the local practice and purchase the vehicles from the lowest bidder. We recognize that there is a legitimate purpose in supporting a local business and its local employees. Perhaps service for the cars will be closer at hand with some saving, and thus you could purchase the automobiles from the local dealer, satisfying the purchase based on what will be saved in the future when the cars need service.

The real dilemma here is where you should draw the line. If you do not have to purchase from the lowest supplier—and under appropriate circumstances, we believe you do not—what criteria should be used in the selection process? Clearly, local preference is permitted. There should be some limits to that, however, particularly where price is concerned.

Generally, whereas sole-source procurement is an invitation to anticompetitive practices—and sometimes waste or even fraud—some products or services are frequently purchased through sole-source procurement. This is particularly true of professional services and technical or scientific products.

Then, too, there should be some limits on the circumstances under which the lowest bidder is rewarded with the contract solely because it is the lowest bidder. Perhaps you are familiar with the story of the astronaut who was in the space capsule, 60 seconds from launch. "How do you feel?" asked the mission-control officer. The response was, "How would you feel if you were sitting on top of ten billion dollars worth of explosive rocket fuel and components, each of which were manufactured by the lowest bidder?"

Answer to Question 10

Will you fire Hazel for borrowing money from petty cash? This is a tough one, and what makes it particularly difficult, at least for us, is that Hazel has actually committed two offenses—she borrowed the money *and* she wrote false receipts. It is the falsification of the records that troubles us the most. Although from a monetary point of view, the falsification of the receipts presents a similar "loss" to the government, we believe the offense is of a different nature and that official receipts should be accurate and valid.

You may also wish to consider what you will tell your supervisors, if you do not dismiss Hazel and she later embezzles $100,000, when they find out you did not fire Hazel on this occasion.

Employees like Hazel, however, are hard to find. No, we would not fire her. But we would reprimand and probably even suspend her. We would also remove the petty cash from her assigned tasks.

Answer to Question 11

Do you resign as chair of the contract source selection board for the procurement in question? As noted in Chapter 6, the federal government has published complicated regulations concerning when and under what circumstances an official has a conflict of interest with respect to an ongoing procurement and postprocurement private sector employment. Here, there is no "revolving door" problem—private sector employment following public service—but, rather, a "reverse revolving door," or public service following private sector employment.

Regardless of the direction in which the door swings, the problem is the same: the private-sector contact creates an appearance of impropriety in the procurement process. Therefore, we believe you must resign as chair of the Source Selection Board and resign from the board. Your resignation, however, may taint the remaining members of the board if they learn the specific reason for your resignation. Thus you must resign for "conflict" reasons without announcing the specific conflict in question.

Finally, we believe you should admonish your former employer from making any similar contract with you in the future.

Answer to Question 12

Do you accept the honorarium at the Sunday brunch? The only reason you were invited to speak at the brunch was because of the experience you have gained as a public official. Thus we believe you may not accept the honorarium. At the executive level, there is an expectation that you will share information you have gained with professional colleagues. We believe you should accept only expenses, that is, mileage, parking, and so on, at a previously understood and customary level. If local rules permit it, and assuming no tax benefit to you, we would support a system that permits you to accept the honorarium and contribute it in its entirety to a local charity of your choice.

Answer to Question 13

Do you pay for your coffee and danish? Civil servants provide a service for which they are paid. If you were to accept the gratuity in question, why shouldn't others, such as the postman, the bus driver, and the garbage collector? Whereas a cup of coffee and danish may not, in some people's eyes, constitute a bribe, it has been demonstrated that small acts of corruption set the stage and lead to larger acts of corruption.

Answer to Question 14

Do you promote Henry? If based on his performance evaluation, Henry is qualified for the promotion, he should be promoted. Promoting Henry reinforces the fact that you expect ethical behavior on the part of your employees. Of equal importance, managerial positions should not necessarily be filled by the most popular member of your staff.

Again, you may disagree with some or even all of our answers to these ethical dilemmas. We believe ethical people can disagree with respect to the answers, and our only advantage (at least we think it is an advantage) is that we have thought about these questions for a long time, and we have heard the thoughts of many public officials concerning the appropriate responses. We do not suggest that our answers are the only right ones or that we are always right.

There are ethical dilemmas far more complicated than the ones we have asked. Some have occurred to us, but we did not present them here because they do not lend themselves to reasonably short explanations, and some of them raise more questions than they answer. Most of all, however, this was not an ethical test but rather an inquiry in pursuit of evidence that what is right or wrong, ethical or unethical, is not always obvious and sometimes requires reflection, thought, and hard choices concerning imperfect solutions.

Are you curious about how you did? We have provided an Ethical Dilemmas Answer Score Sheet as Appendix A. You can score yourself and determine whether or not you are an ethical government practitioner.

Hard choices should concern us. Sometimes, even among the most ethical of us, the easy way out is chosen. What we explore next are the reasons given for unethical practices.

2

Motivations for Unethical Practices

THE CONCEPT OF PUBLIC SERVICE

The man from this large eastern city's inspector general's office was approaching retirement. He had come to city government in the late 1930s and had progressed through the merit system to a senior-management position. During a break in the day's seminar activity, he said he was sad that he was leaving government. "Not because of the usual reasons," he said. "What I'm said about is the complete reversal in the attitude of most of the public and many of my colleagues about working for the government. When I started," he continued,

it really meant something to be a government worker. You were called a "public servant" and felt proud to be called that. Now, when you tell people you work for the government, you get a funny reaction almost every time. I've had people say things to me like, "Oh, you're retired at full pay!" or "Don't want to do real work, huh?" Back then, bright young people opted for public service to a far greater degree than now. It's really sad.

He shook his head. "The really upsetting thing, though, is the attitude of many of my coworkers. Many of them act as if they are the role models those people are talking about."

The attitude of this disenchanted government employee is mirrored by the steady decline in confidence our citizens have in American institutions. The pollster Louis Harris compared ratings of our institutions at three base points across 20 years for 1966 and 1973, 1984 and 1985, and 1986. From 1966 through 1986, three institutions have been held in relatively high regard. They are higher education, medicine, and the military. However, medicine fell from 73 percent in 1966 to 33 percent in 1986. University presidents fell from 61 to 34 percent and the military from 61 to 36 percent.[1] A similar drop in confidence was reported for other leadership types such as the Supreme Court, organized religion, television news managers, and the presidency. They comprise the middle layer of leadership as perceived by the public.

Harris also reported that confidence levels in the executive branch of the federal government (not including the White House) dropped from 41 percent 20 years ago to 18 percent in 1986. Leaders of Congress were rated at 42 percent in 1966, 9 percent in 1976, and 21 percent in 1986. State and local governments never have achieved a higher confidence rating than 30 percent, with state governments rated at 19 percent and local governments at 21 percent in 1986.[2] It is clear from these results that "a sense of mediocrity has been too amply rewarded in far too many institutions in the U.S. over the past two decades."[3]

The highest level of federal employee reflects the low Harris survey results. A 1985 study of the career members of the federal Senior Executive Service (SES) reported that 62.9 percent of former SES members responding would advise or strongly advise someone beginning a career to enter the private sector rather than the public sector.[4] This was the case despite the fact that many former SES employees enjoyed their jobs. According to the 1988 report, *Civil Service 2000*, the public's esteem for the civil service has plummeted. The report states:

Over the past two decades a succession of political candidates has campaigned against "waste in Washington." These candidates often equated the problems of government with the unresponsiveness or incompetence of civil servants. Gradually, this drumbeat of criticism has transformed traditional public skepticism about the government into a mood of outright disdain and hostility. As public esteem for public employment has eroded, fewer of the most talented individuals have entered government service. This has left the government to hire what some have suggested, only half jokingly, is the best of the desperate.[5]

Civil Service 2000 also stresses that low pay and low prestige have been exacerbated by outdated management practices and needless aggravations. The report cites ceilings on career advancement opportunities, random drug testing, drab and seedy work environments, being sent home to wait for another congressional budget fiasco, and other practices that drain energy, initiative, and risk taking and lead to "going by the book" and staying out of trouble.[6] The picture hasn't gotten better this past quarter century.

Back in 1973 there were two national surveys on people's attitudes toward corruption. In one, data were collected as part of the Urban Observatory Program funded by the U.S. Department of Housing and Urban Development. The question asked was, "In some cities, officials are said to take bribes and make money in other ways that are illegal. In other cities, such things almost never happen. How much of this sort of thing do you think goes on in (this city?)" Sixty percent of the respondents thought corruption was serious or somewhat serious. The ten cities in which the data were collected were in the largest 25 at the time.[7] In another Roper poll the same year, 58 percent said that "most" or "fairly many" people in government took payoffs.[8]

In 1976 and 1977, researchers . . . examined corruption problems, searching through more than 250 newspapers for reports of corruption incidents from 1970 through 1976. The newspapers searched reported 372 incidents of corruption over the period. . . . There is no way of telling how many more incidents would have been found if all 1,700 newspapers had been examined, nor is there any way of telling how many incidents occurred that were never reported. Certainly, however, newspapers pay more attention to the misdeeds of high officials than to those of petty bureaucrats, and are more likely to report big-ticket scandals than nickel-and-dime payoffs.

Corruption is not confined to one area of the country. Incidents were reported in 103 cities and in all states but North Dakota, South Dakota, and Hawaii. The Northeast accounted for 97 cases, the North Central Region for 130 cases, the South for 100 cases, and the West for 45.[9]

Almost three-fourths of Americans are dissatisfied with the levels of honesty and standards of behavior in America, according to a poll by *U.S. News & World Report* and Cable News Network. A 1986 Gallup Poll reported that two-thirds of our citizens are dissatisfied with the ethics and morality of others.[10] Contributing to this dissatisfaction is the tenfold increase in indictments and convictions of federal officials for unethical and illegal acts within the past 15 years. In 1975, 53 federal officials were indicted and 43 convicted for these acts. In 1985 the numbers increased to 563 indicted and 470 convicted.[11] By Election Day 1988, 138 Reagan officials had been the subject of official or criminal investigations. An unlucky 13 were convicted, and the countdown continues. In the Nixon administration 21 people who worked for the pardoned president were charged with crimes related to Watergate alone, with 17 convicted. These people faced charges growing out of illegal wiretapping, obstruction of justice, burglaries, illegal campaign contributions, and the like. The Reagan body count is less crude and has been typified by charges growing out of personal enrichment, favoritism, conflicts of interests, and violations of disclosures about investments and income.

Leon Jaworski, the special prosecutor for the Watergate break-in and cover-up, documented more than 90 convictions of individuals and companies in his book *The Right and the Power*. The Watergate and related trials surfaced one illegal and unethical practice after another, leading to President Nixon's resignation and more than three years of trial headlines. The litigious litany contributed to and reinforced the public's negative perception of politicians and government officials.

In October 1988, Colorado Congresswoman Patricia Schroeder (D) prepared a revised "Index to Clippings of Alleged Ethics Violations and Other Improprieties by Reagan Administration Appointees."[12] The index focused on charges of unethical conduct and covers 261 individuals, some of whom were charged for more than one violation or impropriety. Included in the index summaries are the following allegations of unethical conduct, including convictions:

- Acceptance of gifts from a foreign country while serving on the White House staff
- Spending government funds on personal office furnishings
- Involvement by the chief of staff of a Cabinet member in the award of a noncompetitive contract to a former research assistant
- Use of government stationery and mailing frank to hundreds of people on the commission's mailing list to announce that the official was starting his own management business
- Double-billing travel expenses to the White House and the Republican National Committee by an executive assistant on the White House staff
- Failure on the part of a former director of the Central Intelligence Agency to list more than $250,000 in investments, $500,000 in liabilities, names of 70 legal clients, four civil suits against him, and foundations on whose board he served on his financial disclosure forms
- A Justice Department executive employee taking paid leave of six weeks to study for the bar exam
- An assistant to the president convicted on three counts of lying to a grand jury and the House subcommittee that investigated his lobbying for possible ethics law violations leading to a suspended three-year sentence and a $10,000 fine
- A regional administrator of the General Services Administration receiving a two-year prison sentence after pleading guilty to charges of conspiracy and misapplication of bank funds in connection with his embezzlement of more than $213,000 from a New Hampshire bank while he was the bank's vice-president
- A deputy secretary of the Commerce Department negotiating a sale of weather satellites to COMSAT at the same time he was negotiating a high-level job for himself with the same company
- The director of an agency allowing contractors to use government funds to throw parties for the agency's employees
- The chief of staff of a federal department pleading guilty to felony charges related to more than $55,000 in kickbacks he received through government speechwriting contracts and a charitable foundation he created

The index covers almost every conceivable unethical practice and appointment category in the Reagan administration. It also summarizes unethical practices by family members of these government officials on a personal or business basis where government funds supported travel and living expenses or significantly influenced government decisions to the benefit of family businesses or postgovernment employment.

A study by two University of Nebraska political scientists, reported in the *Congressional Quarterly*, found that more than three-quarters of the U.S. representatives who faced ethics charges between 1968 and 1978 were reelected and that even though the charges lowered their winning percentages between 6 and 11, in most cases the members' districts were safe enough that they survived. "We found that being accused of some kind of corruption, whether a morals charge or financial impropriety, did have some impact on members' reelection chances. . . . But in many cases they had real safe seats, so you would have had to have a major swing against them to get them booted out."[13]

The 1988 national elections saw a number of House seats contested on the basis of unethical practices by incumbents. In Rhode Island, Rep. Fernand St. Germain (D) lost his seat after documents unsealed by a federal judge showed that a Justice Department investigation into his dealings with banking industry lobbyists had found "substantial evidence of serious and sustained misconduct."[14] St. Germain previously survived a lengthy House Ethics Committee investigation that found he had violated some financial disclosure rules but recommended no punishment. In Georgia, Rep. Patrick Swindall (R) lost a bid for a third term after his indictment the month before the election and after his indictment by a federal grand jury on 10 counts of perjury concerning his involvement in a federal sting operation aimed at laundering drug monies.[15] Republican Joseph Dio-Guardia lost his House seat because of charges of improper campaign financing. Rep. Mario Biaggi (R), although convicted on 15 counts in the Wedtech Scandal, polled 29 percent of the votes in New York City's 19th Congressional District.

Rep. Roy Dyson (D) won reelection to his seat on the Eastern Shore of Maryland by less than 1 percentage point despite damaging reports about his ties to defense contractors, the suicide of his controversial chief aide, and a federal investigation of his campaign finances.[16] Since his first election in 1980, Dyson majorities averaged almost 65 percent in previous campaigns. In

1984 he won Harford County in his district by 5,600 votes. In 1988 his lead dropped to less than 800.[17] A similarly close campaign in Florida for the seat held by Rep. Bill Chappell, Jr. (D), was won by his Republican opponent after disclosure of Chappell's alleged involvement in the Pentagon procurement scandal. The margin of defeat was less than 1 percent.

The Watergate scandal, coupled with the Carter and Reagan campaigns focusing on "government as the problem," has contributed significantly to the negative perception Americans have about government employees. The daily litany of reported unethical behavior in the public and private sectors in recent years has reinforced for many the attitude that what is reported reflects "the way it is," the rule rather than the exception. Many elected and appointed officials read about or watch the news bites detailing the S&L scandal; the Irangate fiasco; the Deaver conviction; the Boesky stock manipulations; the Department of Defense "Ill Wind" and Housing and Urban Development contracting scandals; the removal of federal, state, and local judges from office; the Wedtech convictions of members of the U.S. House of Representatives; the convictions of county commissioners and city department heads; and so on. Their public response decries the reported behavior. For many, however, their private comments decry the fact that they were caught, not the act itself. For these rascals, their perception of government employment is participation in a smorgasbord of spoils. Their problem is not with the violation of the public trust but figuring out what they can take from the variety of offerings on the spoils buffet without the risk of indigestion and possible terminal career illness of prosecution and conviction.

It is not surprising, given the pandemic of public officials' unethical practices, that in a May 1989 poll three out of four Americans said:

• Members of Congress will lie if the truth hurts them politically.
• Senators favor special interests over the needs of the average citizen.
• The majority of members of Congress improperly profit from office.[18]

The same poll asked respondents to rate the level of ethics and honesty of eight categories of occupations. Their responses are given in Table 1.

Table 1
Level of Perceived Honesty of Eight Occupations (May 1989)

OCCUPATION	EXCELLENT/GOOD	NOT SO GOOD/POOR
Politicians	30%	70%
Members of Congress	39%	59%
Your member of Congress	69%	29%
Members of the news media	62%	36%
Average person	69%	30%
Doctors	72%	27%
Lawyers	39%	59%
Business executives	44%	55%

There is an inherent and puzzling contradiction in the results of this and previous polls and the fact that 98 percent of House members have been returned to their seats in the 1986 and 1988 congressional elections. Sixty-nine percent of the respondents to this poll reported that they rated the level of ethics and honesty of their member of Congress as "excellent/good" and rated other members of Congress 30 points less—39 percent.

Recent experience demonstrates that penalties handed out to public officials for their unethical acts reflect to a considerable degree the bell curve of power. When Rita Lavelle, formerly of the Environmental Protection Agency, was indicted and convicted of lying to Congress, for example, she received a six-month prison sentence, in addition to a $10,000 fine and the requirement of performing community service. She was a middle-level agency manager. When former presidential aide Michael Deaver was indicted and convicted of multiple counts of lying to Congress, he received a $100,000 fine and a three-year suspended sentence. High-priced legal counsel does smooth the furrowed brow of Justice and reinforces the old Middle-European saying that "petty thieves are hanged; major thieves are pardoned."

The public also has to contend with acts such as the veto by President Reagan in 1988 of a bill to amend the 1978 Ethics in Government Act. The bill attempted to close loopholes restraining members of Congress and executive branch members from taking jobs as lobbyists immediately upon leaving government service. The bill's major revisions are as follows:[19]

- Included members of Congress and congressional staff in the act's provisions.
- Extended the 1978 act's lifetime ban on lobbying on a specific matter on which the former official was "personally and substantially" involved while in government service to include "aiding and advising" in addition to lobbying.
- Extended the ban for the top 73 federal officials (i.e., Cabinet secretaries, senior White House staff) from contacting their former agencies for one year to contacting other presidential appointees anywhere in government.
- Added civil penalties to the 1978 act's criminal sanctions, which would have provided an easier-to-prove option for prosecutors.
- Specifically banned any government employee from any postemployment contact for one year regarding a trade negotiation in which the employee participated.
- Eliminated "compartmentalization" of the White House, in which the White House has been subdivided into numerous "agencies." This means, for example, that a former White House official in the press office can lobby the national security adviser. The Government Accounting Office reviewed this practice by the Executive Office of the President (EOP) in 1987 and commented that "several of the functions of the units within the EOP provided by the Counsel to the President do not themselves appear to support a conclusion that they are all distinct and separate entities."[20]

The press reported the reasons for the president's veto, which the president claimed "would discourage talented people from entering government."[21] Reagan left office maintaining his Teflon qualities relative to the scandals that pervaded his senior appointments and his vetoing of congressional attempts to close the very loopholes that have led to abuses by his appointees and further contributing to the negative attitude about the desirability of public service. The veto, and its accompanying message, carried with it the perception that qualified people will not seek public service unless they can gain more than is inherent in the responsibilities of the government job itself. In this context, public service becomes self-service.

If the goal of public service becomes getting what you can while the getting's good, there are no ethics to consider. If the unethical practice under consideration seems to offer a return far in excess of the probability of being caught or the penalty far less than the return, by all means commit the unethical act. If caught, get the best legal defense you can buy and run the string of legal machinations to get the best deal you can. Two prime examples of this credo involved the two highest public offices in America.

Spiro T. Agnew, vice-president of the United States, was spared a trial and a likely jail sentence for unethical practices by resigning and pleading *nolo contendre* to a single charge of tax evasion. Richard M. Nixon, president of the United States, did not suffer the shame of a jail sentence as did more than 50 of his advisers or aides in the wake of the Watergate scandal. A grand jury voted unanimously to name Nixon as an unindicted coconspirator, and the U.S. House of Representatives voted to impeach him. Nixon resigned. Gerald Ford, sworn in as his replacement, pardoned him. Arguments can be made on either side as to whether or not plea bargaining in Agnew's case or the pardon in Nixon's were appropriate or if the judicial process should have been carried out to its ultimate conclusion. These actions on behalf of our two highest public officeholders further contribute to the public's perception that no level of public service is free of unethical practices and that the higher you go, the better deal you can negotiate.

The disparity in sentencing between "white-collar" criminals and "others" is well documented in favor of those who can afford top-priced, creative legal counsel—no court-appointed public defenders for these highest officeholders or their appointees; no time served in penal institutions holding other, less fortunate felons. The perception by the public that there are, in fact, two separate judicial systems is well supported by the disparity in the more favorable treatment of high (major) officeholders.

WHY DO THEY DO IT?

The question of why they do it never surfaced in exactly this way in all of the seminars and workshops we conducted across the country during a three-year period. The question finally was raised in conversations with members of the mayor's cabinet of a large eastern city in preparation for a workshop on ethics in government practice. The workshop was attended by the mayor's cabinet, administrators of major city departments, senior managers, and special assistants to the mayor. Rather than lecture, the question was put on the table for discussion. What follows is not a justification for unethical practices, although the reasons often are used to rationalize improper or illegal acts. This discussion summarizes some of the major reasons given by others to provide a base of understanding for the proactive and reactive solutions to unethical practices discussed in subsequent chapters.

People commit these unethical acts for many reasons, reasons as varied as greed or ideology. Defenses for why they do it range from being under the influence of alcohol or of medication for existing medical problems such as high blood pressure, professed or real ignorance of the law, personal reasons, or any of at least a dozen other reasons. The reasons are similar to those given by nongovernment employees for unethical acts they commit in business transactions or in the normal conduct of their day-to-day affairs. This is not surprising. Government employees reflect a cross-section of the general public. We would expect them to have the same standards and be prone to the same temptations as all of us. Acceptance of public employment, however, puts new factors in the equation—confidence in the integrity of government and ethical practice on the part of elected, appointed, and career officials. After all, no one dragged these officials to their jobs and forced them to work there. Like it or not, public employees are bound to accept the Old Testament admonition, "Do not pervert Justice or show partiality. Do not accept a bribe, for a bribe blinds the eyes of the wise and twists the words of the righteous" (Deuteronomy 16:19).

Let's look at the major reasons for commission of unethical acts that have surfaced during the past few years, most of which were identified by elected, appointed, and career officials serving at all levels of government.

Good Intentions

Government employees frequently become frustrated at the slow pace of getting something done in their agency. They want to expedite what they perceive as something valuable in the best interests of the community. "So, what's wrong with cutting some red tape? There's nothing in it for me, personally, and the job needs to get done. So, we bend the rules a little. Government's supposed to help, right?" Wrong. Maybe. Wrong. Right. In that order. Sure, government's supposed to help, and maybe the job needs to get done, and maybe there's nothing in it for you, and maybe there's too much red tape. But no one individual is empowered to ignore statutes or overrule existing policies and procedures because it looks like the right thing to do.

Many government employees get worn down by a seeming ponderous and snail-like bureaucracy. The rules and regulations appear to erect too many barriers to getting anything done in a reasonable time frame. "The inherent frustrations and constraints of large bureaucracies have been compounded . . . by limited advancement opportunities, needless aggravation, and, often, poor working conditions."[22] For some, short-cutting or ignoring required procedures is okay because it helps people out. Acts of commission or omission due to good intentions cover many unethical, improper, or illegal acts, including less than thorough review of required data or references for contracts, cursory or skipping review of background references for new hires, and making inappropriate decisions on grant or contract awards because the group or individual is "deserving."

The Department of Housing and Urban Development scandal that broke in the summer of 1989 illustrates a creative use of good intentions as a reason for committing an unethical act. Marilyn Louise Harrell, an escrow agent for HUD funds, became known as "Robin HUD" after she admitted that she diverted as much as $5.5 million for what she said were charitable causes.

The ethical way to deal with a perceived or actual moribund bureaucracy is to effect change by recommending improvements in the way it operates. Admittedly, this may be difficult and take time. Cutting corners, however, good intentions notwithstanding, makes you part of the problem. Working to improve the government process makes you part of the solution to the problem.

Ignorance of Laws, Codes, Policies, and Procedures

"I didn't know that" or "I didn't know I couldn't do that" are excuses used by public employees when confronted with a violation of a legal requirement, code, or agency policy or procedure. More often than not, this excuse is used to explain nondisclosure of a situation that may have or did affect an agency decision. Or the situation may not have had any affect on a decision but a violation occurred anyway. This could range from unreported meetings with vendors under consideration for contracts to sharing with a spouse or relative confidential information on an investigation in process. Despite clear regulations governing areas such as acceptance of free meals, travel paid by private sector firms regulated by the agency for which the employee works, or tickets to major sporting or entertainment events, government employees will go along with the offer. Frequently, when reprimanded, the employee will reply that "I can't be bought with a free meal or a ticket to a pro football game." This response avoids dealing with what the employee's jurisdiction requires and, just as important, what the appearance of the free meal or ticket conveys.

One reason offered at a seminar on ethical government practice for not knowing what is appropriate ethical behavior was the inability to keep up with the blizzard of memos, rules and regulations, and other "bureaucratic administrivia." One agency employee listened to another explaining to a third a revised procedure for reporting potential conflicts of interests. "How do you know that?" the listener asked. When told the information was circulated last week in a memorandum to all employees, the response was, "Well, that's what you get for reading all that stuff!"

Ego Powertrip

Look no further than the Iran-Contragate Senate hearings in 1988 for an exemplar of this rationale for unethical practices. What clearly was demonstrated by at least two of the key military witnesses was their stated belief that they were doing what they "knew" the president wanted done. Oliver North, one key witness, acted as though our Congress represented Soviet interests by rejecting military aid to the Contras. He ventured that dealing with the Iranians was a relatively easy matter compared with acts of deception essential in dealing with Congress.[23] North and fellow witness Admiral Poindexter appeared convinced that they knew best and were doing the right thing—this despite the shredding of potential evidence, the admission of lies, and clandestinely funding foreign military operations prohibited by Congress.

Greed

Michael K. Deaver, President Reagan's former deputy chief of staff, was sentenced to a suspended three-year term in September 1988 and fined $100,000 for lying under oath about his lobbying activities after he left the White House. The government's presentencing memorandum submitted by independent counsel Whitney North Seymour, Jr., stated: "The proof during the trial of the Deaver case revealed a pattern of cynical exploitation of the government process as a vehicle for private gain. Witness after witness described the easy road to riches from buying and selling 'access' to government officials."[24] Deaver dropped his appeal of conviction in February 1989 stating that he was tired of being a captive of the system.

Some 20 convictions of members of Congress, presidential aides, and others resulted from investigation into a wide-ranging influence-buying scheme involving the Wedtech Corporation.

By their own account, top Wedtech executives bribed union officials, paid consulting fees and gave stock to politically connected consultants, forged government invoices and faked the books. They made illegal campaign contributions. They looted the companies assets, receiving more than $24 million from stock sales, and more than $13 million in salaries and kickbacks.[25]

U.S. Representative Mario Biaggi, senior member of New York City's Congressional Delegation, was convicted of 15 counts of wrongdoing and resigned his seat. Five other defendants, including a former Bronx borough president, Biaggi's son, and the former Wedtech president who was once praised by President Reagan as a "hero for the 80's," also were convicted.[26]

In a major public health and hospital system in the Midwest, attending physicians whose salaries were paid in full by the system submitted and collected on Medicaid and Medicare bills from the state and federal governments for "services rendered" in the system's wards and clinics. When confronted by the executive director, their response was to threaten a strike. Armed with details, the executive director calmly discussed the consequences of the unethical practices. No strike was called, and the unethical and illegal practices stopped.

It Comes with the Territory

During the height of political "bossism," there were certain understandings about what rewards could be expected from appointment or election to local, state, or federal jobs. In the twenties and thirties about a dozen political machines dominated some of the largest cities and counties in America. Included were Mayor Frank "I am the law" Hague of Jersey City, Tom Pendergast of Kansas City, Ed Crump of Memphis/Shelby County (Tenn.), Mayor James Michael Curley of Boston, and a succession of Tammany Sachems from New York City. At the state level, Huey "I'm the constitution around here" Long ran Louisiana like his own personal fiefdom. Gene Talmadge, as governor of Georgia, decreed laws without going through the state legislature, fired elected officials, and threw workers in concentration camps when they went out on strike. In Duval County (Tex.) the Parrs, father and son, "ran a tight, wretched dukedom populated by illiterate, cringing Mexicans living in appalling squalor and fear."[27] Similar political machines existed in Polk County (Tenn.), Albany (N.Y.), Atlantic County (N.J.), Philadelphia, New Orleans, St. Louis, Minneapolis, Cincinnati, Chicago, and San Francisco. These machines by no means were the only corrupt ones. To some degree they reflected the territorial imperative and expectation of financial reward beyond the salary for the job concerned in many hundreds of other government jurisdictions across the country.

The bosses in these jurisdictions controlled awards of contracts, appointment to jobs that had high-income possibilities through kickbacks and illegal bribes for overlooking building and other code violations, insider information on where new highways and other public construction was to be built, and protection money for illegal activities such as prostitution, gambling, and narcotics. In these jurisdictions the bosses worked hand in glove with the private sector to keep real estate taxes low. They steered insurance business to their own or favored underwriters. They channeled federal monies to expand their patronage and favor certain construction companies in building various public works.

In the Reconstruction period following the Civil War, the archetypal crooked boss was William Marcy Tweed. Thomas Nast, the brilliant political cartoonist, publicized this 320-pound Tammany Sachem, who died in prison after he and his lieutenants stole more than $20 million in New York City funds. One Tammany district boss, part of the "Tweed Ring," succinctly explained what he called "honest graft" as a territorial benefit.

There's honest graft, and I'm an example of how it works. I might sum up the whole thing by sayin': "I seen my opportunities and I took 'em." Suppose it's a new bridge they're going to build. I get tipped off and buy as much property as I can that has to be taken for approaches. I sell at my price later and drop some more money . . . in the bank. It's honest graft, and I'm lookin' for it every day of the year.[28]

The top levels of Tammany thought "honest graft" was their due. They looked down their noses at 'dishonest graft" generated by protection money for allowing prostitution, gambling, off-track betting, violations of health and safety codes, and other illegal activities. Their "honest graft" mentality continues to the present as "white-collar" crime, influence peddling, and the "revolving door" phenomenon.

The examples cited earlier about Wedtech and defense contracting and the dozens of examples of influence peddling and other attempts to cash in on elected or appointed positions underscore the continuing practice of cashing in on one's territorial imperative. The name of the game has changed, but the game keeps attracting new players.

Friendship

"Hey, there's nothing wrong with it. I'm just helping a friend. I'm getting nothing out of it." In one small city, for example, it was common practice for city-owned vehicles and equipment to be used by city employees on weekends and holidays to earn extra money. For example, small cement mixers were borrowed to pour patios and driveways on private property. The bags of cement and sand also were "borrowed" from the city—all of this because the men were buddies with their supervisor who looked the other way. In another city, competitive bidding was circumvented by approving purchase orders for a friend of the head of the purchasing department for $999—one dollar under the amount ($1,000) that would have required such bidding practices.

In one country, the supervisor of the copying room at an agency was approached by an employee and asked to run off 1,500 flyers to be distributed at a local shopping center to recruit youngsters for the Little League soccer teams. A few months later another 1,500 were run before the basketball season starting and in the spring another 1,500 for the baseball season. Everyone admired the supervisor for his civic spirit. No one asked who was reimbursing the agency for the reams of paper paid for by the taxpayers ostensibly to be used for city business. After all, what are friends for?

Ideology

This is a tough one. There's some element of ego trip here. But in this case there is a much deeper political ethos, and the ethos may be a pure ideological belief and commitment. Where the ideology slips across the line to unethical practice is the point at which established practice of government is violated. Ideologues sincerely believe that history will prove them right. Ideologues also believe that their convictions are above the law. The dialogue between Lt. Col. Oliver L. North and George Van Cleve, minority counsel for the committee, during testimony before the Senate Iran-Contra Committee on unethical practices of the executive branch, is representative of the ideologues' assurance that any means justifies getting what they know is the "right outcome."

Van Cleve: You've admitted before this committee that you lied to representatives of the Iranians.

North: I lied every time I met the Iranians.

Van Cleve: And you admitted that you lied to General Secord with respect to conversations that you had with the president? Is that correct?

North: In order to encourage him to stay with the project, yes.

Van Cleve: And you admitted that you lied to the Congress. Is that correct?

North: I have.

Van Cleve: And you admitted that you lied in creating false chronologies of these events. Is that correct?

North: That is true.

Van Cleve: Can you assure this committee that you are not here now lying to protect your commander in chief?

North: I am not lying to protect anybody, counsel. I came here to tell the truth.[29]

Reviewing this dialogue, one can't help but remember the old adage, "If it looks like a duck, waddles like a duck, quacks like a duck, it sure as hell ain't a turkey!" The interesting aspect of this exchange is that Senator Van Cleve was viewed as a "friendly" committee member to North.

Ideological considerations concerning the Reagan and Bush administration's stance on abortion colored decisions for scientific jobs. The chancellor of Washington University in St.

Louis, a medical doctor, withdrew his candidacy as director of the National Institutes of Health (NIH) when it became known that Bush White House officials were going to probe his views on abortion and fetal-tissue research. The ideological litmus test often imposes a political chill on senior-level government executive candidates when the primary attention should be on science. At issue here is filling the most important and influential biomedical leadership role in the world. The director of NIH manages the world's largest biomedical research effort sponsoring projects that range from fundamental inquiry into the secrets of the cell and its components to massive medical-clinical field trials to evaluate the efficacy of new treatments for chronic and degenerative diseases. Loyalty issues based on unresolved ideological positions not only offend well-qualified candidates but also create a situation in which "loyal" but lesser qualified candidates will be appointed to discriminating roles with short- and long-term impact in our nation's health.

Personal or Family Gain

J. David Navarette finally had enough. An engineer in the Department of Energy's Rocky Flats nuclear weapons plant, he rebelled after being forced to work on three sets of plans for a retirement home for the supervisor of a shop where models of nuclear weapons were made. Some 4,000 unauthorized items were made in this shop between 1968 and 1985, including a $15,000 hardwood staircase; a grandfather clock; gold, silver, and bronze medallions; plaques; gold and silver-plated jewelry; a $30,000 wine press; pen and pencil sets; and a $38,000 still to produce wine made for a supervisor at the Department of Energy's facility at Lawrence Livermore. According to testimony before the Subcommittee on Environment, Energy, and Natural Resources of the House Committee on Government Operations, between 1982 and 1985, 2,900 ounces of silver were withdrawn from the Energy Department's strategic stockpile to be made into medallions. The silver was intended for use in the nation's nuclear weapons. The silver was billed to Lawrence Livermore for less than half the world market price, as documents introduced at the hearing showed.[30]

Justice Department spokesman James L. Cole called another unethical practice the largest theft of government property by an individual. He was referring to William John Burns, an Agency for International Development (AID) financial supervisor who pleaded guilty to embezzling $1.2 million in government funds. Burns took advantage of weak internal controls at the AID, where he acted both as disbursing officer and auditor for travel accounts. Burns was certifying officer for payment on all vouchers processed by his section. He was able to create vouchers, certify them for payment, and then cause the U.S. Treasury to issue checks to an alias he created. Burns used the money to purchase an expensive home, jewelry, a satellite dish, and cars.

In this category of "why?" we also can place the many public officials who accept payment for turning away from code violations and accepting payments for overlooking illegal acts. The Chicago *Sun-Times*, in partnership with the Chicago Better Government Bureau, set up a sting operation called Cafe Mirage. The purported owners of this bar and grill set up a video camera at the back of the cafe to videotape conversations with inspectors from the fire, health, and building departments. The results, which were aired on CBS's "60 Minutes," showed a crass disregard for the most blatant code violations following payments of specified amounts in unmarked, sealed envelopes. In fact, the payoffs were so well orchestrated that a certified public accountant was recommended by one of the inspectors as someone who "could give you good advice on what to pay who."

Postemployment "Revolving Door"

In 1988 a major Defense Department contractor scandal surfaced alleging that many of the largest Pentagon contractors fraudulently collected millions of dollars more than they were entitled to. A significant part of the reason is contained in a study of the "revolving door" from the government to the private sector conducted by the General Accounting Office (GAO). The GAO conducts audits of management for Congress to determine, among other things, if the other two branches of government are implementing laws as intended by the legislative branch. The GAO concluded:

this information shows that some individuals leaving DOD and going to work for defense contractors may give the appearance of (1) not having acted in the best interests of the government because they viewed a defense contractor as a potential employer; (2) taking advantage of insider contracts to the detriment of the government; or (3) influencing contract decisions to obtain later employment. We estimate that about 26 percent of approximately 5,100 former high and mid-level DOD personnel had responsibilities while at DOD for defense contractors for whom they later worked. Further, we estimate that about 21 percent subsequently worked on the system, project, or program for a defense contractor that they had worked on while with DOD. In addition, we estimate that about 7 percent were responsible for DOD contracts that later supported their post-DOD employment. We estimate that about 32 percent of the 5,100 have been in one or more of these three situations.[31]

In March 1988 another GAO report said that most middle- and high-level Pentagon officials are ignoring a law requiring them to report their subsequent private employers.[32]

Postemployment conflict-of-interest law does not prevent government employees from accepting employment with firms with whom they dealt on behalf of the government but restricts certain representational activity. This statute, for example, permanently prohibits federal employees from representing private clients before the government on any matters in which they participated "personally and substantially." Former government workers also are barred for two years from representing private clients on any matter over which they had "official responsibility." Certain other restrictions include personal appearances before the government on any particular matter involving specific parties in which they personally and substantially participated while in government, and for one year after leaving federal service, some senior-level employees may not represent anyone other than the United States by making any oral or written communication before their former agency.[33]

A similar problem has plagued federal regulatory agencies. These regulatory agencies are the watchdogs for the myriad, detailed regulations that govern things such as license renewals for radio and television stations, banks and savings and loan institutions, trade and tariff levees in imports and exports, oil and gas production, and other private-sector activities whose revenues add up to billions each year. A real problem facing appointments to these agencies' policy boards is finding someone expert in the regulatory field who would be concerned without compromising decisions he or she might make favoring the appointee's own company or the industry being regulated. All appointees know that following service on a regulatory board, their value is increased to their previous employer and others in that industry.

The revolving door problem is compounded by the exquisitely detailed Federal Acquisition Regulations (FARs) governing the development and purchase of weapons systems, the complexity of legal action in weapons-system procurement cases, the classified nature of the material concerned, the often symbiotic relationship between the Pentagon and the contractor, and political pressures from the administration to spend appropriations in support of foreign-policy initiatives.

The "incentive" portion of the "opportunity-incentive-risk" formula assumes overriding precedence for some in situations in which the rewards are as great as they can be and the risks relatively small in government programs such as defense contracting, zoning, highway construction, other capital construction, cable television, and major service contracts. The revolving door phenomenon inherently involves either the perception of or an actual conflict of interest. In either case, it negatively impacts the government and the public.

Financial Problems and Pressures

In early 1989 there was an attempt to raise salaries of top federal officials and members of Congress by 50 percent. The attempt was defeated following a loud public outcry. Among the bargaining chips used by Congress to persuade Americans that they recognized problems with the honoraria and other income from outside sources was their elimination. Eight years ago, the General Accounting Office concluded that reporting of income and gifts by members of Congress was lax. The GAO recommended random audits of its members' reports after its sampling of 1979 reports filed by its members and their top staff aides. The GAO's audit showed that 43 percent of the House reports and 70 percent of the Senate reports contained errors or omissions. The errors or omissions were identified by the GAO even though they previously were reviewed and accepted by the House and Senate Ethics Committee staff. Among the discrepancies uncovered by the GAO eight years ago was "income with no corresponding asset reports . . . asset but no corresponding income reported . . . creditors were not identified."[34]

The issue of appropriate pay for government representatives is not one of ethics. The issue is political in that the public must make a judgment call on what is equitable compensation for this wage-earner category. The public's judgment is colored by its sense not only about the worth of a job but also by its perception of who is doing (or has done) the job. Given the continuing and increasing "sleaze factor" in contemporary politics, it is small wonder that the public overwhelmingly is against pay raises for government employees. They just don't believe they will get what they are being asked to pay for. As a result, legislators, under the pressures of maintaining two households and other duplicative expenses, have adjusted the legal ground rules concerning outside income and campaign contributions for relief. Also, as a result, they have expanded the opportunity for unethical practices.

Honoraria have represented one significant solution to the expense of maintaining two households for our elected members of Congress. According to Common Cause, House and Senate members accepted some $9 million in speaking fees in 1988. Heading the list of top honoraria givers was the Tobacco Institute with $123,400. Senators receive speaking invitations from more interest groups than do representatives and fare better, on the average by about $10,000, than their House counterparts. Senate members also get to keep 40 percent of the fees compared with 30 percent for the House.

Political action committee (PAC) support figures are substantially higher. Federal Election Commission data through the end of 1988 reported that Senate incumbents and challengers collected more than $50 million in support of their campaigns. The PACs support candidates because they expect a favorable reception for the particular position the PAC membership holds regarding pending or current legislation. Despite claims of neutrality and the ability to vote for what is best for the country, the public's perception is that any politician can be bought. Congress has yet to address the serious special-interest ethical problem represented by PACs.

In response to the overwhelming pressure about honoraria and its potential for unethical decisions on legislation, the House of Representatives passed a pay-raise ethics bill at the end of 1989. The intent was to ease financial pressures and its attendant real or perceived ethical problems. The bill substantially tightened rules for House members on sticky issues such as financial disclosure, gifts, privately paid travel, honoraria, outside income, and disposal of unexpended, accumulated campaign contributions. The salary and ethics provisions of the legislation apply to specific levels of government including members of Congress and their staff, federal judges, and government executives in Levels I through V (Senior Executive Service). The major provisions of the law are:

- House members and all federal employees are banned from accepting honoraria starting in 1991. House members and their staff can give speeches, but the amount they receive cannot exceed $2,000 per speech. The fees can be donated to charity provided the member of Congress or his or her family does not gain any tax advantage. The previous provision of no limit on the total amount of honoraria that could go to all charities was kept in the new legislation.

- Outside income for House members and staff is limited to teaching, with approval of the supervising ethics office, but service on boards of directors must be on an uncompensated basis. In addition, members and staff cannot be employed by a professional services firm or practice a profession for compensation.

- Members, employees, and all noncareer federal employees above GS-15 cannot earn income that is more than 15 percent of the executive level II rate starting in 1991.

- Gifts of more than $200 from any one source in any one year are prohibited, except from relatives. Excluded are gifts of personal hospitality, gifts of $75 or less, and meals not related to overnight lodging.

- Travel underwritten by lobbyists or other private sources is permitted. Domestic travel by members and their spouses is limited to four days and three nights; foreign travel is limited to seven days and six nights. The House Ethics Committee can give waivers to these limits.

- To prevent conflict of interest problems, top House employees are prohibited from participating personally or substantially in nonlegislative matters in which they have a significant financial interest, specifically in contacts with other government agencies and the judiciary. This provision will be written into House rules and is not in the law.

- More detailed disclosure of travel expenses is required, as is travel reimbursement or gifts over $200. New levels of financial disclosure have been added for "below $15,000" and "more than $1 million."

- Blind trusts are allowed, as before, but changes insure the independence of the trustee, and total trust assets will have to be disclosed by category.

- The sticky issue of conversion of campaign contribution surpluses to personal retirement use will end in 1993.

The changes are for the better. The repeal of campaign fund conversions to retirement funds, however, won't occur until after the next congressional campaigns in 1990 and the presidential election campaign in 1992. This legislation passed by the House is referred to by the members as the "House Ethics Package."

Stupidity

One would think that by the time a government employee reaches the higher levels of management there would be a clear understanding of what is and is not ethical behavior. Assuming that there is a clear understanding about the difference, one has to conclude that certain unethical acts occur because of stupidity. The head and number three man at the federal agency responsible for planning and responding to emergencies and disasters, for example, attended a $250-a-plate reception for then Vice-President Bush at the National Republican Club. Both attended the reception as the guests of one of their agency's contractor's, who later billed the agency for the tickets. A House subcommittee accused the agency head of improperly intervening in agency awards and said he should repay $5,091 for federally funded trips out of the country by his wife. The number three man had more than $70,000 in renovations made at the agency's national training center for use as a residence. Number one and number three resigned.

Other examples of stupid behavior include

- Using government stationery to solicit real estate business and using the government's franked envelopes for return mail
- Using a government chauffeur without authorization for trips to and from work and from Philadelphia to Washington
- Using a government credit card to place nongovernment calls
- Seeking a $500,000 home loan by sending bank mailgrams signed with the title of the official from a major federal loan agency
- Offering $200 goodwill gifts to two reporters at the time the nominee was under consideration for a U.S. district judgeship
- Soliciting business from defense contractors while in a key procurement regulatory position in the Defense Department for a firm to be established by the official after leaving the government
- Using government employees, on government premises, during official duty hours to prepare mailing lists, correspondence, and a budget in connection with a senior federal official's planned campaign for governor of a southeastern state
- During a Senate reelection campaign, the candidate stating that he visited a health club that had "nude encounters"
- A senior federal regional director calling federal employees "cockroaches"

The list could be expanded to cover a wide range of other stupid behavior, but these examples should suffice. The fact is that public service is provided by people. Some people, if not all, do stupid things. We have to expect that some public servants will do stupid things.

Exploiting the Exploiters

Some government employees believe that they are being exploited by their immediate supervisor, the agency for which they work, or the current administration in power. They find the rules and regulations too confining. They may believe that they have not been recognized as worthy of promotion quickly enough. They believe that they get all the dirty jobs. They believe they are exploited. They try to turn the tables and exploit the exploiters in a number of ways.

One way is to "work to the rule." This involves strict adherence to an 8-hour, 480-minute day. It involves doing the minimum possible. It involves never volunteering or demonstrating any initiative. It involves trying to fade into the background and avoiding helping others. It involves being satisfied with a "satisfactory" performance rating. It reflects the comment made about some public employees that they "are retired at full pay." One contractor experienced delays of up to 90 days in being paid for invoices submitted to a local government agency. In tracking the approval process from the client agency through the bureaucracy, it was discovered that the agency cleared the invoice in a week to ten days and sent it to the city finance department for payment. It sat in the in-basket of a financial analyst an average of three weeks before it moved to the disbursement office where checks were cut. The approved invoice could sit there for another two to three weeks before the check was made out. It could take another week or two to get the two authorized signatures and the check mailed.

Playing Games

Some career and appointed officials like to play games to achieve what may be unethical or illegal in the normal course of conducting government business.

Here are some other games played and players against whom penalties were assessed for breaking the rules:

- A former chief of staff, Department of Health and Human Services (DHHS), in his official position, helped create a private foundation from which his wife received more than $30,000. This DHHS executive pleaded guilty to felony charges related to more than $55,000 in kickbacks received through government speechwriting contracts and a charitable foundation he created.

- A former head of the Consumer Product Safety Commission required her chauffeur to wear a uniform and hat. When advised that this was improper, she asked that he wear a suit. When he told her he couldn't afford one, two agency officials chipped in to buy him one.

- A former Director of Health Standards, Occupational Health and Safety Administration, Department of Labor, notified Congress he could not turn over his logs because his "dog had barfed all over them."

- The former secretary of interior, James Watt, misused government funds to pay for two private parties at a mansion operated by the National Park Service. When the GAO ruled that he had to reimburse the government for the costs, he had the Republican National Committee pick up the tab.

Going Along

The battering public servants have taken these past two decades has had the insidious effect on government officials of "not making waves" and going along with unethical behavior of their colleagues and superiors. As long as behavior of others did not affect them directly, and blame could not be attributed to their watch, they remained silent. Carter and Reagan campaigned against the federal bureaucrats in 1976 and 1980. The voters seemed to buy what they were selling—the best government was the least government. That's what the voters got. Inevitably, standards began to fall and, particularly in the Reagan years, behavior was tolerated by our Teflon president that would have led to prompt dismissal in previous administrations.

Career civil servants who tried to protest unethical behavior or talked to reporters faced threats of investigations for unauthorized "leaks" or lie-detector tests. In some cases the bureaucrats' "loyalty" was questioned. It didn't take long for the message to get through that it was best to adopt a "go-along," protect yourself mentality. Career officials conducted their business, not too aggressively, and made sure they didn't make waves.

It's clear now that we paid a big price for this "go-along" mode of public service. The dozens of indictments and tens of convictions and resignations of Reagan appointees reflect the cost we paid. Career officials did not question loudly or aggressively enough to force political appointees to understand the difference between candor and disloyalty. Career officials at the Central Intelligence Agency, for example, were deeply troubled about the secret arms-for-hostages deal with Iran. According to the Senate Intelligence Committee report on the Iran scandal, these officials knew the proposed deal was wrong and couldn't or wouldn't do what was appropriate to stop it. The failure of the O-rings that led to the space shuttle disaster in 1985 is another example of knowledgeable engineers allowing themselves to be overruled by their corporate higher-ups. The engineers had doubts about the O-rings functioning properly at the low temperatures present on launch day but didn't do what was appropriate to insure that the proper NASA officials were informed. They went along.

Similar behavior was demonstrated in the Watergate scandal. At the highest levels of government, in the president's inner circle, illegal acts were planned that the coconspirators knew were illegal. Despite this knowledge, these appointees "went along."

The solution to "going along" doesn't mean that bureaucrats should ignore the political initiatives of the party in power and operate the country as they see fit. It doesn't mean, either, that every time bureaucrats see something unethical that they leak their information to the media. What it does mean is that they should not "go along" with threats of political reprisals when dealing with proposed or actual unethical practices. What it does mean is that political appointees must recognize and act on the premise that political loyalty does have limits. The limits are reached when the demand for loyalty encroaches on what is legal and ethical. The limits were reached by at least two key Nixon appointees—Assistant Attorney General William Ruckelshaus and Attorney General Archibald Cox—who refused to substitute loyalty for going along with Watergate cover-up attempts and were fired as a result.

"I Was Only Following Orders"

This was a prime defense at the Nuremburg War Crimes trials. Defendant after defendant used the excuse "Befehl ist Befehl" (An order is an order) as a justification for atrocities against the enemy military and civilian populations. In the trial of the officer who commanded troops involved in the My Lai massacre of Viet Nam civilians, a similar defense was used. In both, this defense was discredited. American jurisprudence does not accept following an order as a defense when such an order is illegal or believed to be unethical or against the belief system of the person being ordered. What is required is the person concerned saying no. Presiding Judge Gerhard Gesell asked of Oliver North, did you "at any time in this process consider in your own mind just not doing it—saying, just say no, I won't do it?" No, North replied, he hadn't.

The jury in the Oliver North trial returned a guilty verdict on three counts. In one, the jury believed that North helped prepare a false chronology of arms shipments and destroyed certain National Security Council documents, thereby obstructing Congress in its attempt to determine the facts of the matter. Presiding Judge Gesell made it very clear to the jury that it could not acquit North on a defense that he followed orders. The jury's verdict of guilty reinforced the legal principle that such acts are wrong and punishable even if the defendant believed he was acting on the orders of his superiors. Oliver North's sentence branded him as a felon. He was fined $150,000, put on probation for two years, required to give 1,200 hours of community service, and forbidden ever to hold federal office. So much for following orders.

Survival at All Costs

Real and imagined pressures to keep an elected seat in a government law-making body, a judicial system, or executive position has led to significant abuses in the ethical practice of government. The abuses primarily affect and are institutionalized in favor of incumbents in elected offices and perpetuated until they become so pervasive and public that changes are forced upon enabling legislation.

One abuse concerns laws that control the amount of income above salaries and benefits for a seat in a legislative body—U.S. Congress, state legislatures, city councils or assemblies, and county commissions.

A second abuse concerns the franking privilege used by congressional members for statewide or districtwide mailings to constituents. These free mailings are timed to coincide with re-election campaigns and to supplement funds raised for the campaign. In effect, the mailings, ostensibly to provide constituents with information about the good job the incumbent is doing, are additional campaign communications paid for by taxpayers. The incumbent's opponent has no similar franking privilege.

A third abuse is the political action committee process. This perfectly legal system helps incumbents amass huge campaign contributions that almost insure reelection. In fact, 98 percent of the U.S. House of Representatives were returned to Congress in the past two elections. Credit the PACs for that. The fear of losing an elected seat has raised the ante for conducting a political campaign. The campaign for a U.S. Senate seat now averages $4 million. Lobbyists are the interface between special-interest groups and the legislators from whom changes in bills and laws are being sought. The pressures on PAC recipients to serve contributor's legislative needs are difficult, if not impossible, to ignore.

The big ethics question that caused consternation in the Senate beginning in 1989 concerned the role of five senators who intervened on behalf of Charles H. Keating, Jr., a private developer. In 1982 he bought Lincoln Savings and Loan Association of Irvine, California, to finance land development. His activities in purchasing junk bonds to develop land in Arizona alarmed federal savings and loan bank regulators. Mr. Keating sought relief from government scrutiny and contributed large amounts of money to what has become known as the "Keating Five"— Senators John Glenn (D-Ohio), John McCain (R-Ariz.), Donald W. Riegle Jr. (D-Mich.), Dennis DeConcini (D-Ariz.), and Alan Cranston (D-Calif.). The five senators and their involvement in speaking to federal regulators on behalf of Mr. Keating all had cases pending before the Senate Select Committee on Ethics in early 1990. The senators have stated that all they did was what they would have done for any constituent who came looking for assistance in solving a problem. None believe that what each did was unethical. The perception appears otherwise.

What's at stake here is the takeover of the Lincoln Savings

and Loan Association by the newly created Office of Trust Supervision to salvage the dozens of failed S&L's at an estimated
cost to American taxpayers of more than $200 billion. The Lincoln
S&L failure was seized in 1989 and was reported to have losses
approaching $2.5 billion, one of the more costly failures on re-
cord. This bill will be paid by future generations of Americans.[35]
While it may be difficult, if not impossible, to attribute the Keating interventions by the five senators to more than the normal
process of helping a constituent, the PAC and other favorite
charities' contributions remain.

What also remains is the perception of "payoff"—services
rendered for a fee. For example, the Republican National Committee created a select group of Republican donors known as
"Team 100." This was the successor to the Committee to Re-
Elect the President (CREEP) of Watergate fame. As with CREEP,
all you had to do to join Team 100 was donate $100,000 to the
1988 Bush presidential campaign. The Team 100 membership
list, a virtual Who's Who of American Business, includes 66
people in the investment and banking community, 58 in real
estate and construction, 17 in oil, and 15 from food and agri-
culture. Team 100 also includes members of the entertainment,
cable insurance, steel, and auto industries. Almost across the
board, members want something from government, whether it's
a cut in the capital gains tax, permission to fly a profitable airline
route, or a favorable ruling in a trade dispute.[36] In Keating's
case, he was clear about what he expected his contributions to
buy. At a press conference "Keating, the subject of a $1 billion
civil fraud suit by the government, said he hoped his financial
support of the Keating Five influenced them 'to take up my
cause.' "[37]

The PAC funds are used for expenses other than campaigning.
They are used to purchase Super Bowl tickets, to lease cars to
commute to work, and for other noncampaign expenses. For
those elected before 1980, surplus campaign funds can accu-
mulate and be used for personal retirement plans.

Another abuse is the honorarium paid elected or appointed
officials for speeches to groups with interests in tax bills or lu-
crative contracts. There is a high correlation between those invited to speak before a trade or professional association, a

specific corporation, or union and the committee chair or membership of the invitee. In fact, key congressional committee chairpersons can earn up to $250,000 in honoraria a year. Very few members of Congress accept no honoraria. Even fewer decline honoraria who hold key committee chairs.

NOTES

1. Louis Harris, *Inside America* (New York: Vintage Press, 1987): 357–60.

2. Ibid., 258–59.

3. Ibid., 260.

4. U.S. General Accounting Office, *Senior Executive Service, Reasons Why Career Members Left in Fiscal Year 1985* (Washington, D.C.: U.S. Government Printing Office, August 1987): 28.

5. The Hudson Institute, *Civil Service 2000* (Washington, D.C.: U.S. Government Printing Office, June 1988): 29. Report prepared for the U.S. Office of Personnel Management, Career Entry Group.

6. Ibid., 30.

7. D. A. Caputo, *Urban America: The Policy Alternatives* (San Francisco: W. H. Freeman, 1976): 65.

8. T. R. Lyman, T. W. Fletcher, and J. A. Gardiner, *Prevention, Detection, and Correction of Corruption in Local Government: A Presentation of Potential Models* (Washington, D.C.: U.S. Department of Justice, Law Enforcement Assistance Administration, July 1978): 1.

9. Ibid., 1.

10. Gallup Poll, 1986.

11. Mark Green, "Memo To The Candidate Re: Law and Ethics," *Tikkun* 3, no. 3 (September/October 1988): 31.

12. House Subcommittee on Civil Service, October 4, 1989, 28 pp.

13. "Most Members Survive Scrapes, Ethics Troubles in Washington May Cause Little Stir At Home," *Congressional Quarterly Weekly Report* 46, no. 16 (April 16, 1988): 1006.

14. Tom Kenworthy and Jay Matthews, "Democrats Maintain Big Majority in House," *Washington Post*, November 9, 1988, pp. A29, A34.

15. Ibid.

16. Howard Schneider, "Dyson Wins by a Nose, Leaving Opponent Considering a Recount Request," *Washington Post*, November 11, 1988, pp. C1, C17.

17. ———, "Congressional Squeaker in Md. Reflects Voters' Suspicion," *Washington Post*, November 13, 1988, p. 85.

18. Richard Morin and Dan Balz, "Majority in Poll Criticize Congress," *Washington Post*, May 26, 1989, p. A8.

19. A Bill to Amend the 1978 Ethics in Government Act, H.R. 2337 and S. 765.

20. U.S. General Accounting Office, *Ethics Regulations, Compactmentalization of Agencies under the Ethics in Government Act* (Washington, D.C.: U.S. Government Printing Office, February 1987): 3.

21. Lou Cannon and Don Phillips, "Reagan Pocket-Vetoes Stricter Ethics Rules," *Washington Post*, November 24, 1988, pp. A1, A5.

22. The Hudson Institute, *Civil Service 2000*, p. 29.

23. Green, "Memo: To The Candidate Re: Law and Ethics," p. 111.

24. *"United States of America v. Michael K. Deaver*, Excerpts From The Case," *Washington Post*, September 26, 1988, p. A13.

25. Josh Barbanel, "Wedtech: Portrait of an American Scheme" *New York Times*, August 7, 1988, p. E4.

26. Ibid.

27. Alfred Steinberg, *The Bosses* (New York: Macmillan Publishing Co., 1972): 6–8.

28. Ibid., 3–4.

29. Peter Carlson, "The Academy Awards of Untruth," *Washington Post Magazine*, December 27, 1987, p. 34.

30. Fox Butterfield, "Gift Orders Filled in Atom Workshop," *New York Times*, November 6, 1988, p. 22.

31. U.S. General Accounting Office, *DOD Revolving Door, Post-DOD Employment May Raise Concerns* (Washington, D.C.: U.S. Government Printing Office, April 1987): 2–3.

32. U.S. General Accounting Office, *Pentagon Officials Ignoring Law Requiring Them to Report Their Subsequent Private Employers* (Washington, D.C.: U.S. Government Printing Office, March 1988): 75.

33. Section 207 of Title 18 United States Code.

34. Walter Pincus, "Lawmakers' Ethics Reports Often Flawed, Unverifiable," *Washington Post*, February 3, 1989, pp. A1, A14.

35. Helen Dewar, "Going Public: Ethics Counter-Offensive in the Senate," *Washington Post*, March 18, 1990, pp. A6, A7.

36. Jean Cobb and Jeffrey Denny, "Power Politics: Fat Cats, Rich Food and Soft Money," *Washington Post*, March 18, 1990, p. B2.

37. Hobart Rowan, "Let's Say Goodbye to the Keating Five," *Washington Post*, November 19, 1989, p. H6.

3

The Cost of a Bribe

During an address in 1976 at the University of Pennsylvania's Wharton School of Finance, the late designer Buckminster Fuller observed that if you had attended a university in 1900, you would have been unable to enroll in a course called "economics." There were no economists or courses of economics in 1900, Fuller stated, and he went on to predict that in the year 2000 there would be neither economists nor courses in economics. "Our one hundred year experiment with this non-science will soon end," Fuller predicted.[1]

Although it is too early to judge the accuracy of Fuller's prediction concerning the survival of the study of economics to the year 2000, it is clear that his view of history is somewhat distorted. To date the birth of economics to some year after 1900 is to ignore as economists, among others, Adam Smith, John Stuart Mill, David Ricardo, and Thomas Robert Malthus. If Adam Smith's *The Wealth of Nations* (published in 1776), with its long and articulate descriptions of the relationship between free competition and free trade and the growth of a nation's economy, is not a book on economics, what is it? Then, too, one would need to find another science—not economics—with which to label Karl Marx's *Das Kapital*, first published in 1867.

Buckminster Fuller, however, would be proud of us, because we approach the issue discussed in this chapter in essentially noneconomic terms. Rather than try to determine "cost" as a function of goods and services, or even supply and demand, we examine the cost of a bribe in terms of its effect on a community.

The extent of bribery, although inexorably intertwined with most acts of corruption, is unknown. A 1977 U.S. Chamber of Commerce report estimated that annual payoffs for corrupt activities costs about $3 billion a year.[2] Later, the *U.S. News and World Report* placed the same estimate at $5 billion a year.[3] When compared to recent revelations concerning the Department of Housing and Urban Development (HUD), however, these decade-old estimates present what appears to be unrealistically low figures.

During July 1989, for instance, the government took over a bank in Hempstead, New York, after investigators found a $4.7 million discrepancy in funds owed to the Government National Mortgage Association (Ginnie Mae). It was alleged that virtually all of these funds were used to make payoffs in the multibillion-dollar mortgage insurance funds administered by HUD.[4]

The *New York Times* has reported that payoffs in the construction industry in New York City during one year was more than $25 million.[5] Regardless of the totals, millions of dollars in bribes are paid every year, and very few units of local government or communities are without some bribe payments and bribe receipts.

BRIBE SCENARIOS

The cost of a bribe can be viewed in many ways. Assume that your city is undertaking the major repair of a number of streets. Assume furthermore that the city purchasing agent has specified Lockport Dolomite Gravel, which is produced by one local company and has virtually no advantage over far less expensive gravel, and that the more expensive gravel has been ordered by the purchasing agent because of his or her receipt of a $10,000 bribe paid by the gravel company. The city will pay more than $750,000 more for this gravel than it would pay for the less expensive gravel. The gravel company was prepared to pay the bribe because it will make a far greater profit on the more expensive gravel. Indeed, had a less expensive gravel been ordered, the bribe-paying company might not have received the contract to supply the gravel.

The cost of this bribe should be examined from at least five points of view. First is the cost to the city: There is the excess cost of the gravel. The city will pay $750,000 more than it should. This money could be used for other programs and by itself, or in combination with other excess costs, increases the city budget. There are other costs to the city, including loss of credibility in the contract process and the increased likelihood that future contracts will be rigged and will result in bribe payments.

Second, the loss of credibility is very hard to measure. Almost any anticompetitive activity tends to increase costs, but quantifying the exact cost is very difficult. An inability to quantify costs, however, does not diminish their effect. We are acquainted with the managing partner of a very large architecture firm who refuses to bid on contracts in a particular state because of his personal knowledge that building contracts in that state are awarded, in many cases, based on the amount of the bribe paid to a state official and not on the merits or quality of the design.

Third, the cost to the supplier includes the $10,000 amount of the bribe. It also includes the likelihood that future contracts will require the payment of bribes and the uncertainty about the size of future bribes.

The supplier's costs also include the possibility of prosecution. Not only can the supplier be prosecuted for paying a bribe, but because the $10,000 payment will almost certainly appear on the bribe payer's corporate books in a disguised fashion, that is, "general business expenses," the supplier also runs the risk of being prosecuted for filing a false tax return. Implicit in the risks of prosecution are the costs of defense attorney fees, fines, being struck from the list of acceptable bidders on government contracts, and prison. During a time when so-called white-collar defendants are being sentenced to prison terms in far greater numbers than ever before, the "cost" of a prison term is neither inchoate nor even unlikely.

Finally, the cost to competitors who supply gravel to the city includes the cost of future bribes they may have to pay to obtain city contracts. Any such payments present to such competitors the same costs the supplier had when the bribe was paid.

Finally, the cost to taxpayers is the inflation in the cost of public works. This is a difficult cost to quantify but is a real one and, in some units of local government, is very serious.

Assume a different scenario. John Smith is stopped for speeding and pays the police officer who stops him $50 to ignore the violation.

The cost to the city includes the loss of the $50 fine. It also includes the loss of credibility in traffic enforcement and damage to the police department's reputation. Although the $50 revenue loss does not appear to be serious, at least not in terms of the total city revenue, it does not take very many similar bribes to affect traffic enforcement revenue materially within any unit of local government.

The damage to police credibility is also a serious cost. It may be easier to measure than appears to be the case on initial analysis. In the aftermath of civil disobedience in cities throughout the country, a number of studies conducted during the past few years have focused on the inability of local police to diminish or quell a riot despite the use of large numbers of police officers, numerous arrests, and substantial force.[6] Some of the studies have reported a complete lack of respect for the police on the part of urban youth raised in poor neighborhoods. Among the reasons for this lack of respect is that it was not unusual for the young people interviewed to report that for many years, as children, they had observed police officers receive bribes from neighborhood bookmakers, prostitutes, and drug sellers. Thus, years later, when police officers ordered these youth to stop or to halt criminal activities, there was no inclination on the part of the young people to obey the police officers who, in the eyes of the youth, were no better than the purveyors of vice who were part of the daily life of the neighborhood.

Damage to police credibility carries with it, in short, many hidden costs. The cost to the driver who pays the $50 includes the amount of future bribes and the increased likelihood that he will be solicited for bribes in situations other than traffic enforcement. It also includes the possibility of being prosecuted.

Many years ago, during a New York City subway strike, one of us observed a motorist, who had run a red light to gain a ten-foot advantage in a five-mile line of traffic, being approached by a police officer. When asked for his driver's license and registration, the motorist inserted a $20 bill between the documents and handed them to the officer. In the process of the exchange, the $20 bill fell to the street. The police officer told the motorist that he had dropped a $20 bill and added that if the motorist did not get out of the car, pick up the money, and put it back in his wallet, the police officer would stuff the bill down the motorist's throat. This sanction is not what is usually intended by the "threat of prosecution," but the effect is the same.

The cost to other drivers is the increased likelihood that they may be stopped in marginal traffic-enforcement situations in the hope that they will pay a bribe. The cost may also include the likelihood that other drivers will offer bribes even when they are uncertain about whether a bribe payment has been requested.

The cost to taxpayers includes the tax burden of increased law enforcement costs that are not offset by the revenue from fines. It also includes the loss of some control over traffic because the size of the bribe is so much less than the insurance premium increase based on the speeding ticket such that the speeding ticket no longer acts as an incentive to drive within the speed limit. The well-documented relationship between excess speed and traffic fatalities, coupled with the wanton slaughter on our streets and highways, makes this cost very substantial.

THE OPPORTUNITY, INCENTIVE, AND RISK ANALYSIS

In addition to material contained in other parts of this book concerning management techniques to eliminate bribes (Chapter 4) and laws and rules for more effective enforcement standards (Chapter 6), a systemic understanding of how and why bribes are demanded and paid or paid without demand is useful to determine how the effect of bribes can be lessened. In each of the scenarios described above, there is an opportunity for a bribe to be demanded or offered. In all situations in which bribes are paid, some opportunity exists and generally (as described below) the opportunity is great, medium, or small.

Similarly, the incentive for the bribe can be great, medium, or small, and the risk to the bribe taker or payer can be high or low. Therefore, bribes can be classified into the following elements:

• Great opportunity, large incentive, low risk;

• Great opportunity, small incentive, low risk;

• Some opportunity, small incentive, high risk;

• Slight opportunity, large incentive, high risk;

• Great opportunity, small incentive, high risk.

The opportunity, incentive, and risk analysis permits the manager to analyze the likelihood of bribe and bribe opportunities within a department, agency, or unit of government.

In the first scenario described above, for instance, in which the procurement officer orders a particular gravel from a local supplier in exchange for a $10,000 bribe, the analysis is as follows. The opportunity is great. This is particularly so if the procurement decision is discretionary and is not subject to a careful review. Managerial or administrative safeguards would decrease the opportunity. The incentive is large because, by any standard, the size of the bribe is substantial. The risk, which measures the likelihood of detection, appears to be low because the likelihood of the bribe recipient being detected is low.

In summary, when there is great opportunity, large incentive, and low risk, forces are extant that lead to the perfect scenario for a bribe. Conversely, when there is slight or little opportunity, small incentive, and high risk, the extant forces should diminish or eliminate the likelihood of a bribe.

In the second scenario described above, in which the motorist pays the police officer $50 to ignore the traffic infraction, the opportunity appears to be great. Not all traffic stops lead to the issuance of a traffic ticket, and police officers generally have discretion to issue warnings rather than citations. The incentive, however, is small. The size of the bribe is small, and there is no continuing relationship between the motorist and the police officer whereby the police officer's conduct will encourage the motorist to pay bribes in the future. The risk is difficult to assess because it depends on how public the transaction is and the extent to which the policy officer's conduct is subject to administrative review.

Typically, administrative enforcement decisions, whether by police officers, housing inspectors, or alcohol beverage control officials, present great opportunity, small incentive, and medium or low risk. We know of only one proven technique to decrease the likelihood of such administrative enforcement bribes, and that is constant monitoring by officials of these departments of the enforcement regularity of the employees. Sometimes this leads to two inspections of some businesses or surveillance of traffic enforcement officers. Clearly, this is an expensive way for a department or unit of government to insure equal enforcement, and a cost-benefit analysis may be required before such a program is undertaken.

The higher the authority of a discretionary decisionmaker, the more likely the incentive to take a bribe. To the extent that high-level decisionmakers have greater influence over decision making and are subject to less review than lower level officials, the opportunity arises even more frequently than does the incentive. Again, it is difficult to determine the risk of a bribe when the circumstances of the payment are unknown and the relationship between the parties is in doubt.

Then, too, the risk analysis of the detection of bribe tends to be a function of how the local community, and particularly the local prosecutor, views the importance of prosecuting a bribe recipient to the exclusion of prosecuting the bribe payer. It frequently happens that a decision must be made at the early stage of a criminal investigation to give immunity to someone; that is, a person will not be prosecuted for the crime, and thus either the bribe payer or the bribe recipient must be given immunity. Without the grant of this immunity, a bribe payer or bribe recipient will refuse to testify against the other party. Absent strong independent evidence that can establish both the payment and the receipt of the bribe, it is impossible to prosecute both the payer and the recipient of a bribe.

In summary, a decision has to be made about whether immunity should be granted to the payer or the recipient. When the immunity is granted to the public official who received the bribe, it is always inappropriate to permit the official to retain his or her position even if there will be no prosecution. Similarly, when immunity is granted to the private citizen, some, noncriminal sanction is appropriate, such as the loss of a business license or being struck from the acceptable bidders list so as to preclude the person from bidding on future government contracts.

Finally, in many bribe situations in which the representative of a private sector corporation or institution pays a bribe, in the event of detection, the private sector institution disavows any knowledge of payment of the bribe. As a matter of civil law, under most circumstances, an employer is legally responsible for the conduct of an employee. If the employee negligently operates the company car or truck, as long as the employee is acting within the scope of his or her duties, the employer is legally responsible for the negligent conduct.

The same standard should be applied when a bribe is paid. Stated differently, private sector institutions should be responsible for policing the conduct of their employees and for making sure that the business ethic of the institution is taught to all who are employed by it. When a private-sector organization instructs employees that their careers within the organization will be enhanced based on a measure of their productivity, the organization must also instruct employees that bribe paying leads to automatic and immediate dismissal.

By imposing sanctions on a private sector organization for the criminal conduct of its employees, the private sector organization will be encouraged to train and police such employees in an appropriate manner.

The bribe scenarios described above assume a bribe has been paid in the ordinary sense of the word; that is, money or something of value has been given to a public official under circumstances in which requesting the payment, offering the payment, giving the payment, and accepting the payment are each a violation of the criminal statute. Unfortunately, under some circumstances, requesting, offering, paying, or receiving money or something of value is not a violation of the criminal statute even when the money is given to a public official.

During 1989 the media reported that bank failures, particularly in the savings and loan and thrift industry, had, under some circumstances, been accompanied by attempts on the part of public officials to interfere with regulatory and enforcement agencies, the activities of which might have prevented or at least ameliorated the failures. In one case, as noted in Chapter 1, five United States senators attempted to prevent a bank regulatory agency from closing an institution that many months later was forced to close because of illiquidity. The activities of the senators may ultimately have cost the taxpayers hundreds of millions of dollars.

Although elected representatives are expected to assist constituents who are being treated unfairly by the government, the "assistance" should not include conduct the appearance of which is inappropriate. In the case of the United States senators noted above, the principal stockholder of the banking institution in question had contributed thousands of dollars to the reelection campaign of each senator and openly boasted that he expected something in return. Note that limits on the amount of money an individual or institution can contribute to a political campaign would do little or nothing to solve the problem described here. Rather, elected officials must be extremely careful—hopefully assisted by a code of ethics—to guard against interfering with legitimate regulatory and enforcement activities even when such activities are directed at a person or institution who or which has contributed substantial sums of money to the elected officials' campaigns.

One practice that might prevent elected officials from interfering with regulatory and enforcement activities would be the requirement that regulatory and enforcement officials and employees be required to report all contacts with them by elected officials or members of their staffs. If the reports of such contact had to be made public on a periodic basis, the frequency of such contacts, we suspect, would be greatly reduced.

Although gifts to political campaigns are a part of the elective process, inappropriate influence by elected officials on behalf of constituents who make such contributions is not part of the elective process.

NOTES

1. From the author's notes taken during the address.

2. T. R. Lyman, T. W. Fletcher, and J. A. Gardiner, *Prevention, Detection, and Correction of Corruption in Local Government: A Presentation of Potential Models* (Washington, D.C.: U.S. Department of Justice, Law Enforcement Assistance Administration, July 1978).

3. Ibid.

4. *Newsweek*, July 3, 1989, p. 21.

5. "The Cost of a Building," *New York Times*, October 12, 1980, p. 19.

6. See, for instance, *Task Force Report: Crime and Its Impact—An Assessment* (Washington, D.C.: Government Printing Office, 1973), U.S. Department of Justice, Law Enforcement Assistance Administration.

4

Profiles of Government Practitioners, or the Corrupter, Functionary, and Ethicist

GOVERNMENT PRACTITIONERS DEFINED

Government practitioners come from all walks of life and, therefore, reflect the full range of ethical or unethical behavior we observe on a daily basis. Most people believe they act ethically, and perhaps they do. As we have seen, however, public opinion polls and newspaper accounts clearly tell a different story about how public officials and corporate executives are viewed by the public. Defense contractor collusion with Defense Department officials, Department of Housing and Urban Development (HUD) influence peddling, the Oliver North conviction, the Meese-Wallach relationship, private-sector scandals in commodity trading, savings and loan industry bankruptcies, and junk bond and insider trading illegalities in the stock market all contribute to the public's perception that "rip-off" is the name of the game in the executive, judicial, and legislative branches of government, as well as in corporate board rooms, offices, and plants.

If there were no standards against which to measure immoral, illegal, or unethical conduct, we would continue our lives in blissful ignorance about government and private sector practices that harm us individually and collectively. The fact is, we do have standards, and those who work in public jobs accept these standards when they accept a government position. The private sector obsession with the "bottom line" to the exclusion of everything else above the bottom line is, in its own way, the profit maker's ethical dilemma. The immorality of increasing profits through mergers and takeovers, with no resulting services or products and with loan defaults and bankruptcies, is viewed by many as a major reason that the United States has lost so much ground in economic competition with Japan and West Germany.

The inherent and continuing danger to the U.S. form of government by unethical and corrupt practices was sharply delineated by Benjamin Franklin more than 200 years ago. "There is no form of Government but what may be a blessing to the people if well administered. . . . This (government) is likely to be administered for a course of years, and can only end in Despotism as other forms have done before it, when the people shall become so corrupt as to need despotic Government, being incapable of any other."

The concept of government serving the public good, the public interest, is fundamental to the ethical practice of government. Government practitioners whose conduct is based on an absence of ethics or an indifference to ethics or who view ethics in relativistic terms do not serve the public good or the public interest. A belief system that is ethically value based will result in behavior that is in the public's interest and serves the public well. Even though value-based ethics may result in mistaken conduct, that conduct never is corrupt.

Three patterns of conduct can be identified that delineate elected, appointed, and career government practitioners—conduct based on no ethics, represented by the *Corrupter*; value-neutral or relativistic conduct, represented by the *Functionary*; and conduct based on ethics that promote the public good and public interest, represented by the *Ethicist*.

Conduct Based on No Ethics: Or, the Corrupter. The Corrupter's behavior is unaffected by ethical or moral commitment. This person is unprincipled and, given the opportunity and enough incentive, will take advantage of every opening for personal gain and profit. The Corrupter's behavior may have the veneer of morality, but as recent televangelists and public officials at all levels have demonstrated, their nonpublic behavior often is something else.

In 1983 an FBI investigation surfaced that focused on the first attempt to clean up systematic corruption in a major municipal court system. Operation Greylord targeted the Cook County (Ill.) judicial system, the nation's largest. Common wisdom at the time believed that nothing much would surface. Anything that did, speculation had it, wouldn't amount to much. If it did, convictions would be difficult and sentences mere wrist slaps. Conventional wisdom was wrong. By 1989, 81 of the 88 judges, lawyers, clerks, and police officers investigated and indicted under Operation Greylord were convicted. Four were acquitted and 2 committed suicide. Charges against the remaining defendent are pending.

One judge was sentenced to six years in prison for taking bribes from a lawyer trying to "fix cases" for his clients, and a jury convicted him of filing false income tax returns. This circuit court judge first donned his judicial robes in 1971. He was the 15th judge convicted since 1983, along with 45 lawyers, 8 policemen, 10 deputy sheriffs, and 3 court clerks. Operation Greylord started in 1981, and for two years FBI agents infiltrated the Cook County judicial network. Undercover agents worked as prosecutors, defense attorneys, victims, and perpetrators. They used James Bond-type concealed electronic devices on their persons, created phony cases, and bugged the judge's chambers. The law enforcement and criminal justice corrupters uncovered in Operation Greylord had disregarded and flaunted judicial decisions, constitutional rights, and human rights and values. All had sworn to uphold the law.

Value-Neutral Conduct: Or, the Relativistic Functionary. This person functions in a neutral way or shifts behavior to accommodate changes in the culture—positive or negative—to keep from making waves. The Functionary doesn't challenge authority even when it's obvious something is wrong is happening. The Functionary "goes along" and "follows orders" even when personal levels of discomfort indicate there's a problem with ethics.

In one unit of the legislative branch of the federal government, there is a recognized problem of alcohol and other drug use on the job. Employees come to work "under the influence" and unable to do their jobs. Supervisors routinely allow these employees to "go somewhere and sleep it off." This government unit has one of the highest accident rates in the federal system. Yet no one connects or takes action about the fact that almost half of all job-related accidents involve alcohol or other drugs. Compounding the problem is the fact that this government unit is considered part of the legislative branch and is not required to meet the same safety, affirmative-action, or other policies and procedures imposed on the executive and judicial branches. Legislators and managers effectively function as value-neutral supporters of a culture that "goes along" and where clear double standards of ethical practice are tolerated.

Conduct Based on Ethics That Promote the Public Good and Public Interest: Or, the Ethicist. This government practitioner believes that there are basic principles underlying the ethical practice of government in a free society. This Ethicist believes, like the biblical scholar Hillel, that you should do to no one that which you do not want done to you. This ancient commentary incorporates the basic tenets of life itself—health, individual freedom, integrity, fair play, and equal justice under our laws. The Ethicist believes in promoting the general welfare and enhancing the public good as an intrinsic goal of a value-based government in a free society.

John Kartak was assigned to an army recruiting station in Minnesota. He discovered that high school diplomas were forged and criminal records concealed to meet that recruiting unit's goals. He called the army hotline and immediately got into water of that temperature. The army ordered not one but two "psychological examinations" on Kartak. One superior even said that Kartak was liable to do something harmful to himself or others because, he said, "I find his behavior highly unstable." Kartak was vindicated when the army's inspector general confirmed his charges and found some 58 people in the Minnesota recruitment office guilty of the charges Kartak reported and additional ones of demanding sexual favors from a female recruit.[1] Apparently, the army's recruiting slogan "Be All That You Can Be in the Army" does not always mean being ethical.

The No-Ethics Corrupter

The Corrupter is a government practitioner whose behavior reflects conduct divorced from a commitment to ethical or moral values. The Corrupter does as follows:

- Engages in unethical or illegal practices, involves others in their commission, or covers them up by lying, shredding documents, or withholding information
- Takes advantage of and makes use of the weaknesses, frailties, errors, and wrongdoing of others to promote his or her own monetary or other gain
- Makes life difficult ("gets those who make waves") for those who conduct themselves ethically or who expose unethical or illegal problems
- Engages in practices to circumvent the law or its intent and to mask wrongdoing or exercises power for power's sake
- Uses the government position and the services delivered as a vehicle for personal gain and increased power
- Views societal problems from a perspective of personal benefit despite waste, inefficiency, injustice, or legislative intent for mandated services to solve them
- Views public needs and outrage about illegal and unethical practices by public officials as irrelevant, uninformed, and humorous
- Sees nothing wrong in manipulating the system for maximum personal, family, or business associate's gain

The Valueless or Relativistic Functionary

The Functionary professes neutrality and behaves that way in the workplace. The Functionary doesn't make waves, doesn't challenge authority even when it's obvious something isn't right, and follows the leader even when personal levels of discomfort indicate there's an ethical problem. The Functionary does as follows:

- Commits no illegal or unethical acts and does not involve others in them but also does not blow the whistle when appropriate

- Engages in no wrongdoing personally or in collusion with others unless there is the potential for great gain at almost no risk
- Does exactly what's expected but nothing more and makes sure that no waves are generated because of an "I don't want any trouble" attitude
- Is concerned primarily with personal or organizational survival and adopts a risk-free posture in the face of ethical problems with coemployees or is willing to sacrifice the whistleblower as a troublemaker or someone who "doesn't understand the way we do things here"
- Provides minimum information asked for and hides information that will show the organization in a negative light, often inappropriately invoking freedom of information regulations
- "Works to the rule" against the public interest by hiding behind and not helping clients understand regulations that are unclear and confusing
- Focuses on data and things (input versus output, cost-benefit ratios, caseload per employee, parking tickets issued) rather than the individuals who are the ultimate recipients of government service's or rather than the quality and effectiveness of services
- Demonstrates "loyalty" by covering for coworkers who arrive late, leave early, need to sleep off alcohol or drug use, or take overlong lunches and breaks
- Views the job as "putting in my time until I can retire"

The Value-Based Ethicist

The Ethicist believes that there are basic principles underlying the ethical practice of government in a free society that should drive public officials' behavior. The Ethicist does as follows:

- Neither commits or involves others nor condones commission of unethical or illegal acts by others or excuses such behavior
- Strives to do the best possible job, leads others in doing the best possible job, and supports advancement based on demonstrated merit
- Goes to bat for those who do their jobs well, supports and protects whistleblowers, and encourages valid employee criticisms by supporting improvements without retaliation for bringing "bad news"
- Maintains open and honest communication, withholding information only when legally or ethically necessary

- Understands the difference between candor and "disloyalty"
- Knows when to say no to a superior when asked to do something that is unethical or illegal
- Serves as a role model in the normal conduct of the agency's business, addressing and responding sensitively, humanely, and positively to the public's service needs
- Insures that the human, fiscal, and material resources under his or her control are applied to maximize the values of life, health, and individual and a free society's needs

It is easy to spot the behavior of the three types of government employees by comparing their behavior when faced with a situation involving use of an official car.

- The Corrupter drives his wife and friends to another city on a Sunday to attend a professional football game. They stay overnight and drive back the next day. The following morning the car is used for an official trip to the next state. The Corrupter submits an expense statement that includes the mileage for the football game trip and per diem expenses for the previous nonbusiness day and claims the mileage and per diem as a business expense when filing his income tax return.
- The Functionary hears about the trip from the Corrupter and how he or she "beats the system." The Functionary keeps quiet and says nothing because it's really not his or her business.
- The Ethicist also hears about the trip and asks the Functionary about it. The Corrupter confirms the incident and invites the Ethicist to the next football game. The Ethicist declines and gives the Corrupter the option of correcting the record or having the incident reported to the Corrupter's supervisor. When the Corrupter declines, the Ethicist reports the incident.

This scenario recognizes the inherent difficulty of achieving significant and lasting changes in the current ethical climate and behavior of the majority of government officials. For a variety of reasons, documented in the Hudson Institute report, *Civil Service 2000*,[2] the phenomenon of government bashing started by Jimmy Carter and raised to a fine art by the Reagan incumbency has contributed to the cowing of government career officials and their adoption of Functionary-like behavior. Presidential appointees in recent history appear to have all but cornered the Corrupters market in the executive branch.

Starting in 1981, for example, the new secretary of the Department of Housing and Urban Development called a meeting of the top HUD career executives. "This is the Board of Directors," he said, pointing to new HUD political appointees assembled in the room. "We make all the policy decisions. . . . You are to carry those orders out. And not ask any questions."[3] Key career officials, including HUD's inspector general, did not criticize HUD's top managers despite documentation of massive management and fraud problems identified in various program audits. Jack Kemp, Samuel R. Pierce, Jr.'s successor, characterized the situation he inherited as "a swamp." Kemp's swamp rapidly turned into a multibillion-bucks-plus bog.

The professional football game scenario above could be prevented and the climate of acceptance turned around with management practices in place in many government jurisdictions. For example:

- *Management Control*: Use of government vehicles outside the jurisdiction's limits must be accounted for by a log that indicates who was visited, purpose of the visit, and the hour the car was returned. The dispatcher must log mileage as the car enters and leaves the garage.

- *Audit Control*: On a random basis, mileage logs of official cars are checked against trip logs of officials to whom cars are assigned. Expense claims are audited for out-of-city trips, on a random basis, plus telephone calls to verify persons visited. Gasoline purchases are totaled by computer according to the car and official assigned to it. Any above-average amounts are compared with the mileage log and trip log.

- *Investigation*: The appropriate investigative unit immediately checks out any report of a possible problem and clears any wrong implication or verifies a problem for administrative and/or legal follow-up.

- *Training*: Mandatory training sessions are held for all officials assigned government cars during which time policy and procedures for their use are explained. The reasons for the policy, to prevent inappropriate use and conserve taxpayer resources, and the controls and penalties for misuse also are explained and discussed. Special situations, such as car breakdowns or commandeering of the car by police for hot pursuit outside of the jurisdiction and how these events should be documented should be included in the training.

Adopting these management practices will prevent abuses of official car use because inappropriate use is much more likely to surface even if no report is made by the person committing the unethical act. Among the poorest management practices are those situation in which, as an office prerogative, no documentation or audit of the use of official cars is required. Chapter 7 discusses these four elements in greater detail.

Tom Fletcher, Paula Gordon, and Shirley Hentzell developed a behavioral typology of the three kinds of government practitioners.[4] Their slightly modified typology provides an analytical framework for matching Corrupters, Functionaries, and Ethicists with their behavior (see Table 2).

"YOU GOTTA KNOW THE TERRITORY"

The opening scene in the musical *Music Man*, takes place in a railroad coach where traveling salesmen are sharing conventional wisdom. What it all boils down to, they agree, is, "You gotta know the territory!" The effective management of the ethical practice of government requires a similar knowledge base. It requires that significant differences be understood and differentiations be made about the three basic kinds of government employees—appointed, elected, and career officials.

There are considerable differences. The career paths for each are different. The demands on them by various pressure groups and job pressures are different. The potential rewards during and after government service are different. The temptations inherent in each career path are different.

Appointed Officials

Appointed officials usually occupy the higher echelons of government in the American tradition of the Spoils System. The mayor, county executive, president, governor, and other executive branch leader has a specific number of jobs he or she controls. Nominations are made to the legislative body for ap-

Table 2
Patterns of Conduct

No-Ethics Corrupters	Value-Neutral or Relative-Ethics Functionary	Value-Based Ethicist
Provides disincentives for truthful and open communication and self-expression leading to the withholding of information or advice likely to prove unpopular or bring disfavor	Focuses on fact, reason, empirically valid "truths," while tending to divorce any concern for honesty and openness from larger societal purposes	Fosters truthful and open communication and self-expression through example, through the setting of a tone, and in other appropriate ways
Provides disincentives for good work	Bases incentive system on a very narrow definition of what constitutes good work	Provides incentives for good work
Constrains the development and contributions of others	Effectively constrains the development and contributions of others	Fosters the development and contributions of others
Sees to it that those who fail to serve in the public interest are removed from the public service if they do not change their ways	Fails to subscribe to a public good concept of the public interest and fails to see any valid way of establishing value-based criteria to determine what is and is not in the public interest	Sees to it that those who fail to serve in the public interest are removed from the public service if they do not change their ways

Uses power in authoritarian, coercive, or Machiavellian ways	Sees power in terms of equity, equalizing power relationships, being more concerned with the fairness of the process than with the human and social purpose served by the process	Sees power as a creative, self-generating force to be used in constructive ways and to be spread, used, and nurtured using educational, normative strategies
Fails to resolve or tries to resolve personal value conflicts ethically and legally	Focuses on process and law in the resolution of conflicts; possible reliance as well on situational ethics	Tries to resolve personal value conflicts ethically and legally and does so without sacrificing integrity
Is guided by primary mentality assumptions of coercion, compromise, and cut-throat competition	Is guided by an imperfect mesh of primary and secondary mentality assumptions	Is guided by secondary mentality assumptions of consensus-seeking, cooperation, collaboration
Plays games with information or withholds or distorts information to circumvent the law, or the intent of legislation; keeps needed information from others in government; keeps information from the public or anyone with a rightful claim to it	Adopts different approaches according to what the traffic will bear	Maintains honesty and openness in the communication of information and withholds information only when legally or ethically necessary

Table 2 (continued)

No-Ethics Corrupters	Value-Neutral or Relative-Ethics Functionary	Value-Based Ethicist
Is disinterested in knowing what is really happening or in developing a real understanding of what needs to be done to protect or serve the public interest	Has no commitment to serve the public interest in the public good sense of the concept; interested in that knowledge and understanding which will assist in maximizing prevailing business values and values of science or of process itself	Is committed to serving the public interest; acts in such a way as to maximize the values of life, health, and individual and societal freedom
Flaunts or disregards judicial decisions, constitutional rights, human rights, human values	Is effectively indifferent to constitutional and human rights	Acts in accordance with the law and with constitutional and human rights
Acts in such a way as to negate, neglect, or minimize the values of life, health and freedom	Effectively acts in such a way as to negate, neglect, or minimize the values of life, health, and freedom	Acts in accordance with the public interest; acts in such a way as to maximize the values of life, health, and individual and societal freedom
Disregards or devalues freedom	Effectively disregards or devalues and undermines freedom	Bases action in a firm regard for individual and societal freedom

Conducts business, delivers services, addresses societal problems poorly, inhumanely, in a value-neutral scientistic way, ineffectively; in such a way as to be wasteful of human, natural, and/or fiscal and material resources; in such a way that science and technology disserve human aims and are seen as aims in themselves

Allows organizational efforts to become characterized by bureaupathology, where process becomes more important than purpose, authority more important than reality, precedence more important than adaptability

Focuses on procedures in such a way as to evade responsibility or to thwart the purpose of the procedure

Conducts business, delivers services, addresses societal problems, as if guided by prevailing business values of productivity and humanism in the service of productivity

Sees to it that organizational efforts focus on process and not purpose, being more concerned with maximizing the prevailing values in business than in serving the public interest

Focuses more on process than on purpose; focuses more on the process of attaining the public good than on the the public good itself

Conducts business, delivers services, addresses societal problems well, humanely, in a human-hearted way, responsively, effectively; in such a way as to conserve valued human, natural and/or fiscal and material resources; in such a way that science and technology serve human aims and are employed in human ways

Sees to it that organizational efforts are characterized by organizational or bureaucratic health, where purpose, service, reality, and adaptability are more important than process, authority, form or precedence

Focuses on purpose, service, reality, and adaptability and on serving the public good

Table 2 (continued)

No-Ethics Corrupters	Value-Neutral or Relative-Ethics Functionary	Value-Based Ethicist
Allows organizational jurisdictions, efforts at policy making, implementation, problem solving, and regulation to become so confused and overlapping as to make the proper conduct of government impossible and the solving of complex problems and the meeting of human and societal needs impossible	Allows concern for process and structure to stand in the way of purposeful action and the resolution or amelioration of complex societal problems	Organizes in such a way that the business of government can be carried out well, responsively and effectively
Is concerned with purpose and service; fails to emphasize the responsibility and obligations of public servants to serve in the public interest	Pays too much attention to process, so much attention that process can become an end in itself; focuses on participation or decentralization in such a way that they become ends in themselves and lead toward "double-democratization," furthering some of the processes integral to a representative democracy but thwarting others -- fails to take into account the problem of accountability and the necessary vesting of responsibility for governmental actions in public servants; focuses on processes thought to insure accountability rather than on the essence of responsibility and public service in the public interest	Makes sure that purpose and service take precedence over process; emphasizes the responsibility and obligations of public servants to serve in the public interest and provides ways of insuring accountability

80

Encourages or takes part in bureaucratic game playing for individual or bureaucratic gain	Refines the rules of the game along scientistically oriented lines, scientism being defined as the divorcing of science, rationalism, and empiricism from human values and concerns	Discourages or avoids bureaucratic game playing for individual or bureaucratic gain
Fails to seek solutions to problems affecting the public interest	Assumes an aggregationist or process-oriented approach to the public interest, not a public-good approach	Seeks solutions to problems affecting the public interest; assumes a public-good approach, being concerned for the preservation and enhancement of individual and societal health
Does not seek solutions because of the possible or expected unpopularity or unwanted consequences of such solutions	Addresses problems when it becomes pragmatically and politically feasible to do so; allows values of effectiveness and efficiency to dominate in the selection of problems to be addressed	Is guided by integrity and a sense of what is right, seeking solutions to and implementing solutions to problems

81

Table 2 (continued)

No-Ethics Corrupters	Value-Neutral or Relative-Ethics Functionary	Value-Based Ethicist
Conducts government in such a way that government fails to be responsive to the public good or it disserves or is indifferent to the public good and emphasizes pseudo-political concerns -- self or narrow group interests, or it is value neutral or nihilistic (without value, purpose, or meaning)	Conducts government in such a way that government fails to be responsive to the public good in that it is not fundamentally concerned with the public good	Conducts government in such a way as to make government be responsive to public needs and to the public interest, and so that government serves the public interest by acting to maximize the values of life, health, and individual and societal freedom while striving to make the best use of resources in accomplishing these aims; emphasizes the political; addresses human needs and problems and humanistic and democratic values essential to a free society and freedom in the world
Fails to act on available information, understanding, and knowledge to avert loss of life and and threats to health and freedoms; fails to act when the solution to convexing societal problem is at hand	Fails to protect and preserve and enhance the public interest through a selective indifference to all of the kinds of information, understanding, and knowledge that bear on the preservation of human values and the solution of human problems	Acts to protect and preserve and enhance the public interest

82

Fails to assume an attitude of stewardship and responsibility for the protection, preservation, and enhancement of human and natural resources	Assumes an attitude of pragmatic expediency or indifference	Assumes an attitude of stewardship and responsibility for the protection, preservation, and enhancement of human and natural resources
Is absent the capacity to meet crises or to anticipate them and prevent them before they arise and failure to develop such a capacity	Pays far more attention to matters of process and structure than to matters of purpose and substance	Develops the capacity to meet crises and to prevent them before they arise
Contributes to a "dog-eat-dog" mode of existence; contributing to the worsening of problems and the weakening of the social fabric	Is implicitly directionless, nihilistic, without long-range goals; generally embraces a disjointed incrementalism unconcerned with any overall developmental goals	Is conducive to a government oriented toward healthy change and development, with those in government serving as change agents and solvers of societal problems
Fails to be responsive to public outcries that government is not serving in the public interest	Focuses on the process of being responsive but fails to be committed to serving the public interest in the public-good sense of the concept	Is responsive to those in and outside government who feel that the public interest is being disserved

Source: From Corruption in Land Use and Building Regulation, Vol. 3, An Anticorruption Strategy for Local Governments (Menlo Park, Calif.: SRI International, January 1978)

proval. Rarely are the nominations disapproved. This is so rare that exceptions receive wide media coverage as in the case of Judge Bork's ill-fated nomination to the U.S. Supreme Court. Appointees can come from either the public or private sectors.

These policy-making and implementation positions are filled from the private sector with people in concert with the executive's political philosophy. They have to pass what political pundits call the "litmus test." Their chemistry has to be covalent with the party controlling the executive branch of government. That's where the nub of the problem often lies.

Appointments from the private sector reflect a pool of business and industry executives who have had little or no experience in the practice of government. They frequently view a political appointment as a payoff for help in the campaign and as a stop along the way to a more important job in government or the private sector. They come to office knowing they will not stay the course and eager to get the job done. The fact that they don't know "the job requirements" is immaterial.

In the recent decades, characterized by Carter and Reagan government bashing, this eagerness to get the job done and lack of government experience has been translated into a negative attitude about how things get done (or do not get done) and impatience with career bureaucrats. The result is that private-sector appointees have been the major group of government officials indicted and convicted in the past twenty years—while in service and shortly after leaving their appointed positions. They have been prominently involved in major scandals such as Irangate, Contragate, toxic waste illegal storage and dumping, nuclear plant safety problems cover-up, savings and loan institution fraud, Housing and Urban Development influence peddling and fraud, illegal Pentagon procurement influencing, and falsifying generic drug application and review processes.

For private-sector decision makers, the inertia of the government bureaucratic process can become unbearable and inappropriate decisions made to cut the red tape. For others, decisions are made to set up their return to the private sector or insure that their trip through the revolving door will land them in the correct executive suite. Career bureaucrats frequently abdicate

their responsibilities because of intimidation from these politically well-connected agency executives. The higher level of those
in government agencies—in federal service, the Senior Executive
Service (SES)—can have their careers negatively affected and
lose significant bonuses if they appear to oppose their superiors'
decisions. The gambit frequently used by political appointees to
quell opposition based on accurate readings of government policies and procedures is the charge of "disloyalty." In effect, if
people are not with you, they're against you. Candor on the
part of an experienced career official that causes discomfort about
a questionable course of action by an appointee can be ego challenging to someone appointed by the chief executive who believes he or she is doing what is right. In effect, you either are
on the team or off.

The only cabinet member to serve throughout the Reagan
administration was Samuel R. Pierce, Jr. During his two-term
tenure as secretary of Housing and Urban Development, symp-
toms of problems at the agency as early as 1982 were ignored.
One writer at that time questioned the unusual number of grants
to congressional districts where Republicans were in close races.
After Pierce left office, investigators at HUD and the Justice
Department found that auditors ignored or failed to monitor
escrow agents who either delayed forwarding sales proceeds for
years after selling HUD property or embezzled the funds. In
fact, the HUD inspector-general issued three internal audit reports that said his investigators could not account for millions
of dollars from property sales.

The HUD problem has been around for more than 25 years.
Former Michigan Governor George Romney, a former HUD secretary, established the Office of Inspector General in 1972 in
response to scandals in subsidy programs for single-family
homes and multifamily rental properties. Problems continued
in the agency, which led to charges about preferential personnel
referrals for HUD appointments. Congressional reports criti-
cized HUD for failing to protect low-income people in projects
insured and subsidized by HUD from real estate agents who
"would inflate property appraisals to earn larger fees, do little
to make sure occupants could service their mortgages, and, fi-

nally, stick HUD with foreclosed properties that weren't worth anything like the amounts for which they had been appraised and insured."[5]

Mismanagement, waste, fraud, corruption, and manipulation of various entitlement programs continued throughout the 1970s and 1980s with millions of dollars in mortgages declared in default that HUD had to make good. No one really knows the extent to which "insiders" benefited from the indifferent oversight of HUD managers in Washington and regional offices. The recent and ongoing scandals in Pierce's administration indicate it could approach $1 billion. In one Georgia project alone, for example, $750,000 was in dispute between HUD auditors and a former Reagan campaign adviser and his partners.[6]

What is clear from the 25-plus years of HUD scandals is that little of consequence probably will be done. Top-level officials apparently did nothing that was illegal. Cronyism is not an indictable offense. Neither is aggressive pursuit by the private sector of funds for subsidized housing that municipalities don't want or are not equipped to pursue. Nor under existing legislation or federal ethics rules is it illegal for former cabinet officials to make a few telephone calls to HUD to earn hundreds of thousands of dollars in consulting fees.

Other questions, however, should be asked. Where were the respective congressional oversight committees when this was taking place? To what extent have honoraria by self-interest groups contributed to congressional support for favored treatment or interference with inquiries into improper practices? Where was the Office of Management and Budget or follow-up to reports of the HUD inspector general? What about performance reviews of top HUD managers? Where were the media that cover the Washington beat? Where were the whistleblowers in HUD?

Andy Warhol, the late artist and commentator on our culture, said that the public's attention span on media events is limited to 15 minutes. Congressional outrage about the HUD scandals seems to have lasted less than a quarter of an hour. Once it appeared that the major players in the scandal were nonprosecutable, Congress shifted to other, 15-minute-or-less media bites.

In the fall of 1989, for the second time in American history, a former cabinet head "took the Fifth Amendment." Pierce, claiming the congressional committee investigating the HUD scandal, which topped an estimated $5 billion, had prejudged the matter, joined the company of Albert B. Fall, secretary of the interior under Warren G. Harding. Fall, a senator from New Mexico before appointment to Harding's cabinet, took the Fifth when asked about a black satchel full of money he had received from an oil magnate. Fall, it seems, had received the money in return for favorable decisions on leases in the Teapot Dome oil preserves in Wyoming for one E. L. Doheny. Fall was convicted of accepting this $100,000 cash bribe. The Teapot Dome Scandal was one of the worst scandals in our history. By the time all of the HUD investigations end, the teapot may well turn into a samovar.

Whatever does fall out from the HUD investigations, the Republican government bashing has become the petard on which they have hoisted themselves. Republicans have held the Oval Office, in part, by campaigning against waste, fraud, and abuse. The HUD situation under Pierce could not have occurred without the complicity and arrogance of the appointees and former appointees in their decision-making jobs.

Elected Officials

Elected officials are in the enviable position of setting and policing their own ethics rules. On rare occasions, usually when the press or a member of the opposition seizes an opportunity to focus on the unethical behavior of an elected official, investigations are undertaken and the incumbent chastised or forced to resign. A recent example of this was the charges brought by Congressman Newt Gingrich against former Speaker Jim Wright for violation of the limit on outside earnings. The charges involved purchase of a book by Speaker Wright by outside supporters in an attempt to finesse the earnings limit from honoraria paid for speeches before private businesses and industries and not-for-profit trade unions and associations. The rules for disclosure of outside income, which require annual reports by members of Congress and their staff aides, were no better followed in 1989 than in 1981. Both studies by the General Accounting Office uncovered errors or omissions by almost half of the House reports and more than two-thirds of the Senate reports. The House, for example, prohibits its members from accepting any gifts that total more than $100 in any year from anyone with a direct interest in legislation—a lobbyist, businessperson, trade unionist, association employee, and so on. The $100 includes meals and tickets to sports events and the theater. The figure for the Senate is $35. Under House rules, however, you don't have to count a meal or ticket under $50. The Senate doesn't count any meals, beverages, or entertainment from a lobbyist or a lobbyist's employer if it doesn't include overnight lodging.

Career Officials

In some ways, the career official unfairly has taken the unethical rap for the appointed and elected official. The "big ticket" scandals during the past twenty years have involved appointees and electees. Career officials commit unethical practices that range from improper use of their telephones for personal or outside business calls to collusion with private contractors to give these favored companies an inside edge on procurements.

Part of the problem facing career officials is the ambiguity that exists among and between the various agencies where career officials come into daily contact with existing and potential contractors. There are rules that govern employee behavior across a wide range of conduct. An example of the problem can be illustrated by the Federal Acquisition Regulation (FAR), Procurement Integrity (48 CFR Part 1, *et seq.*).

In response to serious violations of existing procurement regulations, particularly in the Defense Department, Congress enacted Public Law 100–679, Office of Federal Procurement Policy (OFPP) Act Amendments of 1988. The law involves three key provisions:

- Prohibition of offers of employment to government procurement officials who are involved in the procurement
- Prohibition of bribes and gratuities

• Obtaining or exchanging proprietary data or source-selection data without proper disclosure

All federal agency procurements greater than $100,000 are covered by this legislation. Contractors and bidders must certify to the contracting officers that there are no violations to the law with respect to the specific procurement or make such disclosures as may be appropriate. In addition, it becomes incumbent on the contractor to have each employee who participated personally and substantially in the procurement certify familiarity and compliance with these requirements and report all violations.

Penalties for violation of provisions of PL 100–679 include suspension, debarment, or termination of an award for default; individual civil fines for individuals up to $100,000; and civil fines to organizations up to $1 million.

On March 27, 1989, a proposed rule for PL 100–679 was published in the *Federal Register* (54 FR 12556), and public comments were solicited. Ambiguities identified and clarifications requested included:

• Two indifferent methods were proposed to identify the start date for a federal procurement; in major procurements the date would be published in the *Commerce Business Daily*, and in others the contracting officer would identify in the solicitation the date on which the procurement began. Questions were raised about the confusion of two methods of start dates and whether or not any notification was needed.

• The definition of source-selection documents also was questioned. Exception was taken to categories of information included in source-selection documents and oral discussion of data potentially classifiable as such. There are discrepancies among and between agencies about what constitutes this information.

• The interim rule also included a Catch–22 provision. The rule provides that certain specific information could be source-selection information *whether or not it is so marked*. The answer to this concern is that "all reasonable efforts will be made by the Government to mark this information."[7]

After creating a furor in and out of government, the Bush administration was successful in getting the new procurement-regulation language postponed for one year. A rider was attached to the bill in conference by Senate conferees. Ambiguities continued in this confusing ethical legislative arena. Among them are whether or not the Office of Federal Procurement Policy or the Office of Government Ethics was supposed to write regulations for the law and whether or not anyone who violated PL 100–679 between July 19, 1989, and December 2, 1989, when the old law was in effect, can be prosecuted. Given the unequal application and ambiguities of the situation, it is doubtful if anyone is at risk.

Although it is clear that the government was trying to address recent procurement improprieties in PL 100–679, further bureaucratic and legal proscriptions and penalties will not resolve the need for key behavioral changes on the part of career officials and their respective staffs. First is the example of ethical leadership. At the executive level, if Pierce, Dean, and others had provided ethical leadership, the current scandals would have been substantially prevented. Failing role models at this level, career managers had ample opportunity to raise questions and objections about clear improprieties and illegal practices. Then, too, all HUD staff know there is an Inspector General's Office and hotline. Asserting an ethical stance and climate would have been a major signal and deterrent for the HUD-appointed employees and the industry concerned. Second, had the proactive and maintenance elements of the management process been addressed in a consistent manner, the *ex post facto* investigation or prosecution elements would not have been necessary. These elements are discussed in detail in chapter 7.

The public, however, has the right to ask, "Is anybody watching?" The public views the continuing media din that shifts from scandal to scandal like some undecided hummingbird unsure about which flower to visit to collect the sweet nectar of exposure. The public, as opinion polls report, does not view unethical practices as the particular preserve of Republicans or Democrats. People do not differentiate between the three categories of government officials. The level of government is of little matter. The overwhelming majority do not even follow current, headlined scandals such as those involving former Speaker Wright, James

Watt, HUD, the S&L's, the "Keating Five," and Ed Meese. The public views everyone the same way—with distrust and lack of confidence.

THE "GRAY AREA" COP-OUT

Discussions we have had in our seminars across the country inevitably lead to someone stating that there are "gray areas" where there are no clear guidelines on which to proceed to resolve an ethical dilemma. This is true, the argument goes, for any category of public official. We think this argument not only is a cop-out but a way to focus inappropriately on a problem and its solution.

If we look at the universe of potential dilemmas with which a government employee is faced, the overwhelming majority can be resolved with knowledge about *existing* laws, administrative policies and procedures, and other guidelines extant in the jurisdiction concerned. There are agencies established in almost every jurisdiction to assist employees with resolving potential or actual dilemmas. They include ethics offices, legal counsel offices, ombudsmen, and similar resources. When a dilemma surfaces and the responsible resource cannot satisfactorily respond to the dilemma, that jurisdiction must resolve it as quickly as possible. If necessary, an interim solution should be agreed upon until the longer term resolution is in place, that is, legislative action, administrative memorandum, formal policy, or guideline change. The inherent dangers in deciding a course of action on what appears to be an ethical dilemma is that the person deciding may not have all the information needed for the decision.

Given the nature of the times in which we live, we have to expect that new and challenging dilemmas will continue to surface. The gray areas we did not foresee a decade ago or last year may surface at any time. All three branches of government have a responsibility to address these gray areas expeditiously to prevent them from camouflaging the unethical practices of functionaries and corrupters.

NOTES

1. Molly Moore, "How-to Manual for Potential Whistle-Blowers Sounds a Few Shrill Notes," *Washington Post*, August 25, 1989, p. A19.

2. The Hudson Institute, *Civil Service 2000* (Washington, D.C.: U.S. Government Printing Office, June 1988): 29. Report prepared for the U.S. Office of Personnel Management, Career Entry Group.

3. Bill McAlister and Chris Spolar, "The Transformation at HUD: 'Brat Pack' Filled Vacuum at Agency," *Washington Post*, August 6, 1989, pp. A1, A10.

4. Adapted from T. Fletcher, P. Gordon, and S. Hentzell, *An Anti-Corruption Strategy for Local Governments* (Washington, D.C.: National Institute for Law Enforcement and Criminal Justice, Law Enforcement Assistance Administration, U.S. Department of Justice, September 1978): 48–55.

5. Charles L. Dempsey, "Formula for Scandal," *Government Executive*, October 1989, p. 32.

6. "HUD Seeking to Recover $700,000," *Washington Post*, October 19, 1989, p. A7.

7. *Federal Register*, 54,90 (May 11, 1989): 20489.

5

The Integrity Checklist

What is the ethical climate of your community? How would you
rate the integrity of your state and local government? How do
you arrive at that rating, or stated differently, what are the in-
dicators of corruption, fraud, or a lack thereof?

Several years ago, the U.S. Department of Justice commis-
sioned a research firm to evaluate incidents of corruption in state
and local governments throughout the United States.[1] The firm
decided that the principal investigative tool would be a compilation of newspaper articles about state and local corruption taken
from newspapers throughout the country. Researchers examined more than 250 newspapers for reports of corruption incidents between 1970 and 1976. These newspapers contained more
than 372 incidents of corruption.[2] Although a methodology that
uses newspapers as an indicator is certain to record a local corruption that has been reported in the local press, it does not
record corruption that has not been unearthed by the media or
some other agency, and it tends to overemphasize corruption
in units of government that have an alert media.

Collecting newspaper stories, however, may be as effective a
method as any other to determine the existence and extent of
corruption. It is at least as good as anecdotal reporting, the
judgmental technique that is sometimes employed as a means
of determining whether corruption exists within a local agency
or throughout the local government.

During the workshop sessions at which public officials were presented with training materials about how to maintain integrity within a government (which are more particularly described in Chapter 7), we traveled with several others to approximately 25 cities throughout the United States to present the courses. One of us and another trainer, the late Victor I. Cizanckas, who during the training period and at his death was chief of police of Stamford, Connecticut, would race each other to determine, through the use of their own integrity checklist, the ethical climate in the city they were visiting. Each of us employed about the same technique as described below, but a note of caution: Cizanckas undertook this work with 20 years of police experience and the author in question undertook the work after spending nine years as a prosecutor.

The exercise began at the airport; it was always interesting to see whether we could find evidence of unethical behavior before we reached our hotel. By carefully selecting taxicab drivers—minority cab drivers tend to be underemployed; that is, they are qualified for jobs much better than the one they have, they are frequently more verbal than their nonminority counterparts, and they tend to be very "street smart"—we were able to detect behavior in major cities that raised questions about the ethical climate of the community.

Many taxicab drivers, for instance, were able to tell us (sometimes we operated alone and sometimes we were together) where to place a bet, the location and the hours of operation of a high-stakes poker game, the telephone numbers to call if we wanted a woman in our hotel, and, on some occasions, where to buy drugs. Keep in mind that these inquiries were being made by total strangers.

We did not simply ask questions of the drivers; we engaged them in conversation and asked indirect questions about the ethical climate of the city that in turn led to more direct questions. You may wish to ask yourself some of the same questions about your own community.

- Can you fix a speeding ticket?
- Where can you place a bet?

- Who is the best zoning attorney, and do you rate his or her ability as the best because zoning variances are always granted if that attorney represents the moving party?
- Is there some way to be appointed to a civil service position without taking the test?
- How strict is the housing code enforcement?
- Who really runs this city?
- How extensive is the drug problem?
- Is there any way that I can get a liquor license if I have a criminal record?
- Whom do I have to see if I want to bid on a city contract?
- Is this a good place to live?

Neither Cizanckas nor the author ever purchased drugs or a woman or placed a bet, but once, before reaching the hotel, we were driven to and actually observed a high-stakes poker game in which there were tens of thousands of dollars on the table. On one occasion Cizanckas began to ask some of the questions noted above to a driver who turned out to be a moonlighting police officer. Fortunately, Cizanckas had a badge.

Taxicab drivers are not unique in their ability to sense the presence and extent of corruption in a community. Other sources of information, not necessarily in order of importance, include newspaper reporters, chamber of commerce officials, clergy, lawyers, bar owners and bartenders, law-enforcement personnel, hotel help, officials of homeowner associations, and contractors.

The ability to fix a ticket or obtain a liquor license after conviction of a crime is not necessarily synonymous with official corruption. Applicants with disqualifying criminal records are sometimes awarded licenses; such an award may be evidence of gross negligence, but it is not necessarily evidence of corruption. Similarly, law enforcement officials and high-ranking political appointees are sometimes in a position to dismiss a motor vehicle infraction for a relative or a close friend. Although this conduct may be morally wrong, it is not evidence of widespread corruption.

Show us a community with open and notorious gambling,

however, such that perfect strangers can place a bet or gamble within hours of their arrival, or show us a community with easily available prostitution services in the hotels or a community where it is common knowledge that certain people can insure your receipt of a successful bid on a city contract or a community where whom the zoning lawyer knows is always more valuable than what the zoning lawyer knows, and we will show you a community in which there is very strong evidence of official corruption.

Enforcement of gambling and prostitution laws are, to some extent, a matter of police and prosecutor discretion. Therefore, the existence of some violations of these so-called vice crimes can carry a mixed message. Law enforcement discretion, however, does not include ignoring obvious and public violations of potentially serious offenses. When there is evidence of widespread vice violations, there is evidence that either the police department is refusing to enforce the law for administrative reasons, or representatives of the department are being bribed to ignore such violations.

As noted above, newspaper reporters and the media in general may be a barometer of the ethical climate of a community. Media reports of local government corruption are almost always based on solid facts. Although there are incidents of false media reports of corruption, and although media reports rarely contain sufficient evidence such that a conviction in criminal court can be insured, media reports of corruption are evidence of the existence of a lack of government integrity in a community.

In 1964 the Task Force on Organized Crime of the President's Commission on Law Enforcement and Administration of Justice published an article entitled "Wincanton: the Politics of Corruption."[3] Wincanton was the fictional name of an American city that was the focus of a study that examined the politics of vice and corruption.

Wincanton, the identity of which is known to the authors of this book, was a city that had been recognized for many years by law-enforcement officials as a city with a serious corruption problem. Indeed, the city was so thoroughly corrupt during most of its twentieth-century history that almost without exception law-enforcement and prosecution activities were restricted to work by the U.S. Department of Justice and statewide investigation commissions. Interestingly, as of 1964, no mayor in the history of the city had ever succeeded himself in office. Although some of these mayors were honest and had driven most vice operations from the city, such mayors had always failed in re-election attempts.

The research into the politics in Wincanton was conducted, in part, through the use of interviews with law-enforcement personnel, media representatives, former and active elected officials, and a citywide poll.

As with any city in which vice was open and notorious, local law-enforcement officials protected the vice activities in exchange for bribes. These same officials sometimes supplemented their illegal income by demanding kickbacks on city contracts and by extorting payments from vendors who did business with the city. During all but a few years, the city had a dominant political party, the registered members of which outnumbered the registered members of the second political party by more than two to one.

There were periods of reform in Wincanton during which honest administrations drove the illegal vice activities from the city, municipal contracts were awarded on merit, and personnel decisions were not based on either nepotism or favoritism. As noted below, however, reform administrations were short lived, and vice and corruption promptly returned. One period of reform came to an end during the middle 1950s. As it did, the incoming mayor summoned the old chief of police into his office. The mayor told the chief that that he could not remain in the position of chief, but that he could stay as a police officer as long as he agreed not to enforce the state's gambling laws. The chief told the mayor he would not ignore gambling and said he would "keep on arresting gamblers." The former chief was assigned by the mayor permanently to operate the jail in the basement of police headquarters. This is an example of the extent to which vice and corruption ruled all governmental decisions in Wincanton including personnel decisions within the police department.

Interviews with federal investigators and other knowledgeable informants permitted the authors of the Wincanton study to note

that "two basic principles were involved in the Wincanton protection system—pay top personnel as much as necessary to keep
them happy (and quiet), and pay something to as many others
as possible to implicate them in the system and to keep them
from talking." A modest example of this is reported in the following dialogue between the nephew of the head of the local
vice operation and a newly elected county court judge who was
called shortly after being elected.

Nephew: Congratulations, judge. When do you think you and your wife
    would like a vacation in Florida?

Judge: Florida? Why on earth would I want to go there?

Nephew: But all the other judges and the guys in City Hall—Irv [the
    Uncle] takes them all to Florida whenever they want to get away.

Judge: Thanks anyway, but I'm not interested.

Nephew: Well, how about a mink coat instead. What size coat does your
    wife wear?

In example after example, the researchers documented how the
illegal element in the city corrupted local officials, sometimes
with small presents that became larger presents and sometimes
with initial payments of large presents.

It was hard to separate so-called small corruption from large
corruption. Some local officials made a huge amount of money
doing nothing more than fixing parking and speeding tickets.
Since at that time state law did not require competitive bids,
some local officials made huge sums of money demanding kickbacks from city vendors. As sometimes happens, local officials
in Wincanton developed a hierarchical structure of official corruption, with those involved in certain activities referring to
themselves as recipients of "honest graft," whereas others received "dishonest graft." As the authors noted, Wincanton officials were the quintessential example of the advice given by
state Senator George Washington Plunkitt, a Tammany Hall official in the early part of the twentieth century:

There's all the difference in the world between [honest and dishonest
graft]. Yes, many of our men have grown rich in politics. I have myself.
    I've made a big fortune out of the game, and I'm gettin' richer every

day, but I've not gone in for dishonest graft—blackmailin', gamblers, saloon keepers, disorderly people, etc.—and neither has any of the men who have made big fortunes in politics.

There's an honest graft, and I'm an example of how it works. I might sum up the whole thing by sayin: "I seen my opportunities and I take it."

I see my opportunity and I take it. I go to that place, and I buy up all the land I can in the neighborhood. Then the board of this or that makes its plan public, and there is a rush to get my land, which nobody cared particularly for before.

Ain't it perfectly honest to charge a good price and make a profit on my investment and foresight? Of course, it is. Well, that's honest graft.[4]

Although a quarter century old, it is interesting to note that the Wincanton study contains recommendations to curtail local corruption, including increasing the salaries of public officials; strengthening the civil service position; requiring competitive bidding for almost all municipal contracts; and eliminating the opportunity for extortion and bribery in the guise of campaign contributions. The Wincanton authors specifically rejected an annual audit of city books on the grounds that despite the wide-spread corruption for a long time, the Wincanton books were always in proper order.

Are there any Wincantons today? Certainly. Times have changed, but there are cities that are modern Wincantons. Indeed, perhaps the most remarkable thing about the Wincanton study is the fact that many of the citizens of Wincanton voted against reform mayors in subsequent elections because the incumbents had reformed the city. Under a reform administration, it was no longer possible to enjoy the vice activities that flourished in Wincanton during corrupt administrations. The business community, which knew precisely how to function when municipal contracts were rigged, found it difficult to perform adequately and profitably when the bidding process was competitive. Government officials, who under corrupt administrative knew what the rules were for advancement within public service, became confused when civil service procedures were applied to promotions.

In short, Wincanton experienced long periods of a local government that was thoroughly corrupt because this type of government became the norm. As with most pursuits in life, people became more comfortable with the process they understood and tended to reject the unfamiliar.

INTEGRITY CHECKLIST AND DIAGNOSTIC INDICATORS

Experience teaches that there are laws, rules, procedures, and practices that a community should have in place to prevent and detect incidents of official corruption.

A series of questions are asked below, the answers to which will determine whether your community has the necessary tools in place.

Official Policy toward Corruption

- In your jurisdiction, do statutes and ordinances clearly forbid (and clearly define) bribery, extortion, and other forms of official misconduct? Does your jurisdiction have an official code of ethics specifying what conduct is officially desired and what is officially prohibited?
- Do these rules cover all elected officials, appointed commission members, department heads, and lower ranking employees whose duties may offer opportunities for corrupt acts?
- In addition to prohibiting cash payments, do rules prohibit the acceptance of meals, gratuities, discounts, and favors from any individual or firm doing business with the city or county or subject to regulation by the city or county? Do rules forbid engaging in private business on city or county time or using city or county materials or equipment for private purposes?
- Is outside employment that conflicts with official duties forbidden?
- Are officials forbidden to represent private interests in dealing with city agencies or to take positions with firms they have previously regulated?
- Do campaign finance laws set limits on contributions from individuals or firms doing business with the city or county?

For those questions that you answered yes, additional factors to consider are the following.

- Are all personnel covered by the statutes, ordinances, and rules regularly informed of what is required of them in the conduct of their job?
- Are there mechanisms for detecting and dealing with violations? Does every detected violation result in an appropriate disciplinary action or in prosecution?

A no answer to any question in this subsection indicates a deficiency; the jurisdiction does not have all of the tools needed to combat corruption.

Detection Tools

- Are there laws or does the city or county have ordinances or codes that require officials and employees to disclose conflict of interest?
- Are officials and employees required to disclose special knowledge of or contacts with firms or individuals subject to their authority?
- Are officials required to disclose their assets, debts, and outside employment?
- Are employees required to disclose any outside employment? Is information provided by officials available for inspection by the public and the news media?
- Are records kept of all actions and decisions that might be vulnerable to corruption?

A no answer to any of these questions indicates a deficiency; your jurisdiction may not have the tools needed to detect corruption. If the answer to any of these questions is yes:

- Does the city or county have "freedom of information" laws that guarantee public access to official records and reports?
- Does the city or county have an established mechanism to take complaints from the public and investigate them? If so, are the complainants informed of the results of the investigation?

A no answer to any of these questions indicates that your jurisdiction may not have the tools needed to make detecting corruption easy.

Management Practices

- In recruiting candidates for positions that offer an opportunity for corruption, is information gathered about the candidates' backgrounds, and is that information verified?
- Do training programs for new employees cover integrity expectations and the penalties for abuse?
- Are these policies reinformed in subsequent retraining programs or review programs for those in service?
- Does the city or county have a disciplinary code that specifies policies, penalties, and enforcement procedures for all employees? If so, is the code enforced?
- Are employees charged with ethics violations immediately suspended until the investigation is completed, or can they transfer or retire and keep their pension rights?
- Are the actions of employees regularly reviewed by supervisors, and are the actions of supervisors, department heads, and managers regularly reviewed by the chief elected or appointed official and the board or council?
- Are all employees with decision-making powers required to record their decisions in writing, with their name attached, and to justify any deviation from existing policy?
- Do rules provide penalties for failure to provide information on demand when it is a matter of public record or failure to respond to questions or inquiries about decisions?
- Do rules provide for failure to report a corrupt act observed or failure to deal with an instance of corruption by a subordinate?

Elected and Appointed Officials

- In considering candidates for appointed positions, is information gathered about the background of the candidate, and is that information verified?
- Is there an orientation or training program for newly elected and appointed officials that sets forth what is expected of them in terms of integrity and what the penalties are for abuse?
- Do officials encourage public participation in, or inquiry about, official decisions?

- Are officials required to respond to questions from other officials, from the media, and from the public?

- Are official activities regularly monitored by news media and by citizen organizations? If so, are questionable activities reported to the public?

- When a questionable activity is reported, is the official immediately suspended by the chief executive pending the outcome of the investigation, or is he or she allowed to resign?

- Do local and state prosecutors investigate all allegations of official corruption? Are formal charges brought against officials when improprieties are found?

- When elected or appointed officials are convicted of corruption, are penalties imposed that are substantial?

- Has your unit of local government selected a cable television company? If so, how was the selection made? Were competitive bids received from a number of different companies? Is there a system in place to replace the company that was selected because of its failure to provide adequate service or for other reasons?

- Does your state or unit of local government run a lottery or license off-track betting establishments? If so, who regulates the lottery and how are the regulators selected? Who regulates and enforces the rules of the off-track betting establishments?

Chapter 7 discusses specific practices that governments must employ to prevent unethical practices and maintain ethical ones.

NOTES

1. *Prevention, Detection, and Correction of Corruption in Local Government* (Washington, D.C.: Government Printing Office, 1978). Office of Development, Testing and Dissemination, National Institute of Law Enforcement and Criminal Justice, U.S. Department of Justice.

2. Incidents were reported in all states but North Dakota, South Dakota, and Hawaii.

3. John A. Gardiner and David J. Olson, *Task Force Report: Organized Crime, Annotations, and Consultants' Papers* (Washington, D.C.: Government Printing Office, 1978). Task Force on Organized Crime, The President's Commission on Law Enforcement and Administration of Justice. The study was part of a larger investigation of the politics of law en-

forcement and corruption financed by a grant from the Russell Sage Foundation.

4. William L. Riordan, *Plunkitt of Tammany Hall* (New York: E. P. Dutton, 1963): 3. Quoted in the Wincanton article.

6

Managing the Ethical Practices of Government through Laws and Rules

Sometimes acts of unethical behavior in small and large communities are focused in the Buildings Department. Information about corruption typically surfaces when a buildings inspector is found to have accepted a bribe and, assuming a well-conducted investigation and an alert prosecutor, this act of unethical and criminal behavior inexorably leads to the discovery of similar acts committed by other Buildings Department employees.

Soon, builders, land developers, landlords, and other buildings-industry representatives in the community appear as witnesses before the grand jury or other investigative body or are indicted or both. Sometimes the investigation spreads to the local Zoning Commission. If that happens, the extent of the unethical and criminal behavior and the size of the bribes paid to the government employees are inevitably discovered to be much larger than the bribes first discovered to have been paid to employees of the Buildings Department. This is not because Zoning Commission employees have less integrity or more greed but rather because the amounts of money that representatives of the private sector are prepared to pay to influence zoning decisions are among the largest bribes that are offered to public officials. (See Chapter 3 describing the cost of a bribe.)

Thereafter, the truth or falsehood of the accusations is resolved in the courts through trial or plea, and the question of whether the employees accused of unethical behavior should be dismissed is resolved by the administrative body that determines eligibility for continued public employment. But what seldom occurs—there are a few units of local government in which this is not true—is an investigation by some person or group to determine what went wrong and why and what corrective action can be taken to detect, deter, or even prevent future unethical behavior. All too frequently official corruption investigations are concluded with the conviction or acquittal of the bribe giver or bribe taker.

The public official who is genuinely interested in maintaining an ethical climate for public employees, however, should use the opportunity of a corruption investigation (and its findings) to alter or amend existing management practices or procedures so as to affect future behavior. In fact, when the investigative body has concluded its work, when the plea bargains or the trials are over, when there is no further publicity, some person or group of persons within a department or agency (or even better, in an independent agency) should conduct its own investigation to determine which practices, rules, regulations, or laws should be changed to prevent further corruption. Sometimes this can be done before the unethical behavior allegations have been settled in the criminal courts or the administrative bodies. Stated differently, when the criminal investigation is over, the management investigation should begin.

Prescriptive packages for managers who wish to decrease or eliminate opportunities for unethical behavior are few and far between. This chapter describes certain elements that may prove to be helpful. As noted below, training employees about the importance of ethical behavior and providing them with knowledge about the laws and rules described in this chapter is an essential element in maintaining employee integrity.

LAWS, STATUTES, AND ETHICAL CODES

This book is neither a legislative drafting guide nor a legal textbook. There are many laws, statutes, and ethical codes, however, that have proven to be effective in maintaining employee integrity, and some of them are described in this chapter. Each unit of local government must determine the appropriate wording or structure of ethical rules that can be enacted by the legislative body or promulgated by the chief executive in the state, county, or other unit of government. Thus only a general description of the laws, statutes, and ethical codes that have been proven to be effective in helping to maintain government integrity—and not necessarily in the order of their importance—can be presented in this chapter.

First a word of caution: Laws and rules that attempt to define integrity, judgment, and ethical responsibility must interact with official standards. If they do not, their status may define official morality but will be impractical to and thus will not impact upon the officials to whom they are directed. In addition, laws that attempt to define conduct may produce official conduct that is rule-bound and unimaginative. In short, laws and rules that address the troublesome subject of integrity must be expressed in simple language and should offer examples or case studies.

Among the most well-known rules is "Thou shall not kill." It is not a complicated standard, and it is expressed in simple terms. Its simplicity, however, is illusory. Does it mean that you may never kill? How about self-defense? Are mercy killings permitted? May you kill animals? To raise a subject that is of immediate and intense debate in out society, does the prohibition include a fetus?

In short, laws and rules that define ethical behavior are only one tool to be used in maintaining integrity. It is important, even with the most direct and simplest of laws and statutes, that the prohibition of mandatory conduct described be stated in unambiguous terms, in a way that can be understood by everyone and in a way that does not raise more questions than it answers.

Open Government

The appearance of integrity is sometimes as important as integrity itself. Perhaps because we are citizens of a constitutional republic that permits and even guarantees freedom of choice, we become suspicious of government decisions that are made in secret. Our literature is replete with references to "backroom, cigar-smoking decisions." There are laws that address this problem.

Open-government or sunshine laws have been enacted in many states and communities. Essentially, these laws mandate that all meetings must be open to the public and any official action taken at a closed meeting is not binding.[1] Sometimes, a corollary to the open-meeting law exists that permits people to inspect all government records at any reasonable time.

Meetings held by zoning commissions, school boards, legislative committees and bodies, and—except as described below— virtually all executive departments and agencies should be open to the public. But such an open-meeting policy is ineffective and is in fact a sham unless a mechanism exists whereby the public is informed well in advance of the time and place of meetings. In many instances, open-government legislation requires that such a notice also contain the agenda for the meeting; in such cases, departures from the agenda are not permitted. When a meeting's agenda and the decisions to be made at the meeting may affect a large number of community residents, an open-meeting law should require that the meeting take place in a facility large enough to accommodate the community interest.

An open-meeting law is not synonymous with a law that requires public participation at meetings. Whether such participation is always appropriate is beyond the scope of this book, but participation by the public in governmental decisions, which probably includes the right to be heard on issues that affect the public, goes a long way toward creating at least the appearance of fairness and integrity, not to mention reasoned decision making.

Inevitably, there are meetings of government bodies that cannot or should not be open to the public. Although "closed meetings" should be kept to a minimum, they are a necessary part of government operations. If the city council is considering the purchase of land on which to construct a municipal parking lot, for instance, both the location of the facility and the maximum price the city is willing to pay for the land should not—for obvious reasons—be discussed in an open meeting. Similarly, if a unit of local government is considering the government's position in negotiations with a union of government employees, the personnel manager's settlement authority with respect to wage increases should not be discussed in public. In general, personnel decisions are properly exempt from an open-government statute.

The rationale for any exemption from an open-government law, however, should be obvious. An open-government statute that seemingly exempts all important decision-making sessions from public scrutiny is an ineffective law and may even be counterproductive.

In one eastern state the open meetings law enacted in 1978 contains a catch-all exception permitting closed meetings when "the public body finds" it is "compelling that the general public policy [for open meetings] be ignored." The result is that in one county in the state that has a population of more than half a million, the county council closed 44 meetings during one year. Other legislative bodies throughout the state routinely close many of their meetings. An open-government law that is routinely ignored may create more skepticism in the population than in a state that has no such law.

An open records law also needs certain exemptions. In addition to privacy considerations (personnel records generally should be exempt from public inspection), for example, memoranda prepared by government lawyers for use by government officials where the unit of government or its employees are defendants in court actions must be kept confidential.

Financial Disclosure

A unit of local government that by law, statute, or policy does not require high-ranking elected and appointed officials to file a financial disclosure statement is a unit of local government that ignores the importance of government integrity. Short of a blood test that could identify applicants for public employment who are unethical, there may not be a more effective tool to insure public employment integrity than to require the filing of financial disclosure statements. Many state and local governments require financial disclosure statements.

A financial disclosure statement should require the public official to disclose, at a minimum, all sources of income: any business, partnership, or firm in which the official has an interest of any kind; all sources of income for a spouse or dependent child residing in the official's household; gifts of any kind received during any calendar year in which the official serves; any gift of a value in excess of $50 received by the official's spouse or dependent children; where political contributions are permitted, a contribution of any kind to any candidate for public office; the legal description of all real property the value of which exceeds $2,500 in which the official has a direct or indirect interest; the identity of any creditor to whom the official owes $1,000 or more exclusive of charge accounts or credit-card accounts; and the identity of any financial institution in which the official maintains a demand deposit account in an amount of $1,000 or greater.

Although the disclosures mentioned in the preceding paragraph should be considered as minimum financial disclosures, and although financial disclosures are extremely important, there are two caveats to financial-disclosure laws or rules that should be noted. First, financial-disclosure laws frequently require the public official to use a designated form on which to make disclosure. This form is either described with great particularity in the financial disclosure statute or an independent body develops the form. It is important that the form be as simple and straightforward as possible. We have seen financial disclosure forms that would require even the most sophisticated public official to employ both a lawyer and an accountant to assist in the preparation of the disclosure. One such form presented a definition of "income" that was substantially longer and dramatically more complicated than the definition of the same word that is used in the Internal Revenue Code—and that definition is neither short nor a model of clarity. Financial disclosure forms, in summary, should not require the public official to disclose his or her financial ignorance, nor should such forms be designed to trap the unwary.

Second, it may be appropriate for financial-disclosure forms to be confidential and to be revealed only if allegations of unethical behavior are filed against the public official. Most of us deplore public revelation of our financial condition. Employment as a public official should permit some privacy, and the purposes of financial disclosure may be met if a designated depository contains financial disclosure statements without public access to the statements.

Finally, it is difficult to define which public officials should be required to file financial disclosure statements. Units of government describe upper echelon public officials in many ways. Clearly, any official who is appointed by the chief executive to a cabinet or department position should be required to file such a statement. Beyond that, senior supervisory personnel—depending on the size of an agency—should be required to file statements. Attempts to distinguish between personnel of the same rank based on levels of responsibility and excusing some from filing financial disclosure statements is almost certainly doomed to failure. It is also probably unfair.

Financial disclosure statements of elected officials are described below under "Legal Standards for Ethical Behavior of Elected Officials."

Conflict of Interest Statutes and Rules

Generally, there are two types of conflict of interest statutes. The first is the restrictive criminal conflict of interest statute that prohibits, subject to criminal penalty, enumerated acts. The second and usually much broader conflict of interest statute describes standards of conduct for which administrative action, including reprimand or dismissal and sometimes restitution, is the sanction for a violation.[2]

Although conflicts involving personal financial transactions are frequently the focus of conflict of interest rules—thus underscoring the importance of financial disclosure statements—avoidance of conflicts of interest is far broader than avoiding only conflicts of interest associated with personal finances.

Traditionally, conflict of interest statutes prohibit conduct during the time the official is a public employee and for some time thereafter. The statutes require public officials to make decisions solely on the merits and free of any and all inappropriate influence. When a public official's decision-making authority may be influenced by friendship, family, prior employment, or any other relationship, or may *seem* to be so influenced, the public official should refuse to participate in making the decision. It is important to note that the payment of a bribe or the acceptance of a financial gratuity is not the only act that constitutes the violation of a conflict of interest statute. Indeed, because such statutes recognize the importance of the appearance of ethical conduct, conflict of interest statutes frequently penalize the public official who fails to disclose a conflict or who makes a decision when a conflict exists even under circumstances in which the official's decision is considered to have been made fairly and impartially.

What about the public official whose responsibilities involve a regulated industry or profession and who knows many representatives of the industry or the profession over whom he or she has regulatory authority? Is that person an appropriate individual to head a regulatory department or agency? Stated differently, what about the public official whose strict adherence to conflict of interest rules would prevent the official from making more than a small fraction of the decisions or judgments that are required of the office?

This is a difficult issue, and it is one that has engendered no small amount of debate. On the one hand, it may be that the best insurance commissioner a governor can appoint is a person who has worked in the insurance industry for many years. It is possible that the most qualified Buildings Department director is the experienced land developer. On the other hand, in both cases, the nature of the official's experience would lead the prudent appointing authority to recognize that there are many potential conflicts of interest. Appointing a less qualified individual will decrease or possibly eliminate conflicts of interest, but the sacrifice of knowledge and experience may be intolerable.

Conflict of interest issues can extend to postemployment conflicts by former government officials. That subject is discussed below under "Postemployment Restrictions and Unethical Behavior."

Whistleblowers

During October 1988 a Kentucky jury ordered a large oil company to pay $69 million in damages to two employees who were fired for refusing to pay bribes to foreign officials.[3] During the same month, a Veterans Administration employee received a $10,000 award—for "moral courage"—because he reported that another Veterans Administration employee—who was his superior—beat hospital patients. Unfortunately, however, the employee who reported the beatings was fired.

Whistleblowing—reports by government employees of acts of unethical behavior by other government employees—is encouraged, frequently through the enactment of laws that protect the whistleblower. This encouragement, however, is not infrequently overcome by the routine dismissal of those who blow the whistle. President Ronald Reagan, one of the strongest proponents of eliminating fraud, waste, and abuse at the federal government level, during 1988 undertook a "pocket veto" of legislation that strengthened the rights of federal government whistleblowers.

Even when whistleblowers inform about information that virtually everyone agrees should be reported, they can be the subject of management revenge. A few years ago, the Nuclear Regulatory Commission fined the Tennessee Valley Authority $150,000 for harassing three engineers who had supported a colleague who reported operational problems in a nuclear power plant. The engineers had been treated unfairly in job assignments, performance appraisals, and promotion opportunities after they supported their whistleblowing colleague.

In late 1988 the federal government agreed to pay $560,000 to settle a lawsuit brought against the government by a whistleblower who had been fired from his job as maintenance supervisor for most government buildings in Washington, D.C. This former government official had angered officials at his agency, the General Services Administration, when he charged that the savings the agency officials had claimed to Congress came at the cost of neglecting the condition of many government buildings and creating health and safety hazards. Subsequent investigation showed the former official's complaints to have been valid.

Protecting whistleblowers is the only effective means of insuring effective whistleblowing. Although it is true that some so-called "whistleblowers" are in fact malcontents, many are not, and those that are must be screened at the operational level (i.e., when they blow the whistle) and not in the legislation that protects whistleblowers. Only when government employees are protected from reprisals and believe they will be protected from reprisals will whistleblowing occur. Because department or agency employees are frequently the only people who are aware of unethical acts on the part of other government employees, those who are in a position to observe and learn about unethical acts must have the confidential nature of their informer status protected. Usually, this can be accomplished only through legislation.

The Reagan-vetoed legislation, which was reintroduced in 1989, strengthens the rights of federal whistleblowers in a number of ways. It requires an agency to show "by clear and convincing evidence" that whistleblower retaliation was not a factor in a personnel action. It also prohibits reprisals against employees who cooperate with inspectors general (see the next section), testify before government bodies, or refuse to obey an order that violates the law.

There are limits, however, to the protections that can be given to whistleblowers, particularly those who report government abuses from outside the government. In late 1988, for instance, Raytheon Company, the nation's third largest arms manufacturer, fired a corporate vice-president, Lawrence Korb. This dismissal occurred as the direct result of the secretary of the navy complaining about Korb to deputies who in turn complained to Raytheon officials. Korb, a former assistant secretary of defense, was critical of the administration's defense budget, and his criticism annoyed the secretary of the navy. Korb, who left Raytheon to become a dean at a major university, is an experienced defense analyst and extremely knowledgeable about the defense-budgeting process. His whistleblowing, however, cost Korb his job.

The federal government has established a Fraud, Waste, and Abuse Hotline in many departments and agencies. Although such a hotline undoubtedly increases the number of people who are willing to become whistleblowers—anonymous reports are accepted—a hotline is a waste if meaningful reports are not investigated.

Nancy Kausen, for instance, a federal contracting officer, reported to the Defense Department Hotline that a four-inch stainless steel ring for which the navy was paying $271 contained $.67 worth of steel. The contractor who manufactured the ring later acknowledged that rotor assemblies, of which the ring was a part, were sold to the navy for $6,600 each but should have been priced at $1,500.

Kausen's complaint to the hotline, however, did not produce an investigation. Rather, it was only after she reported her findings to the Pittsburgh press that the Defense Criminal Investigative Service began to investigate the matter. Upon hearing Kausen's story, one experienced military procurement official stated that based on her nine years of experience with federal government hotlines, they appear to be worse than useless.[4]

Inspectors General

Although the responsibilities of inspectors general might better be discussed in the section of this chapter describing codes of ethics, the position of inspectors general within an agency or department is frequently established through legislation, and thus this material is presented here.

By way of example, pursuant to legislation enacted in 1978, the federal government established the Office of Inspector General in each of 12 government agencies (the number has now increased to 19). All audit and investigative activities of each agency (except for special-purpose activities such as enforcement of international agreements and export licensing) were consolidated in the Inspector General Offices. In the federal scheme—and the federal government is not the only unit of government that has inspector generals—the inspector generals are nonpartisan presidential appointees who require Senate approval.

Pursuant to the inspector-general law, an inspector general cannot be prevented from carrying out an audit or investigation or issuing a report or subpoena. Similarly, the inspector general must be given unlimited access to all department records and files. In addition to reporting to the Congress twice each year, the inspector general in each agency reports directly to the department head or deputy but can be fired only by the president, who must advise the Congress of the reasons for the dismissal.

The inspector general reports to Congress must detail any major problems, abuses, ethical violations, and deficiencies identified within the agency during the previous six months, together with recommendations for corrective action. These reports must cite any recommendations for corrective action that were reported earlier but that have not been acted upon. In addition, the reports must describe any inspector general requests for information or assistance that were unreasonably refused. Although a department head may comment on these semiannual reports to Congress, the report by the inspector general is not subject to change or edit by the department head. Inspectors general may make special reports to the Congress about particularly serious problems or flagrant breaches of ethical standards.

Almost without exception, Inspector General Offices in each agency in the federal government maintain a hotline that employees may call (anonymously, if they wish) to report allegations of unethical behavior.

Postemployment Restrictions and Unethical Behavior

Former presidential counselor Michael Deaver was convicted of perjury. He was accused of lying to a grand jury that was investigating whether he had taken improper advantage of the fact he had been an advisor to the president of the United States.

Many units of government prohibit their employees from both "switching sides" and from taking advantage of information (or a title) they acquired while employed by the government. Senior employees in many governmental units, for instance, are forbidden for a period of one year after they leave the government from contacting their former agency or department on behalf of a client or representative in the private sector. Similarly, government employees frequently are prohibited from representing another person or entity with respect to a contract they administered while working for the government. Even stronger conflict rules apply to lawyers who appear in court on behalf of the government.

Laws that require ethical behavior within the government must include restrictions on postgovernment activities. Postgovernment employment restrictions must be carefully crafted, however, so as not to create an undue hardship on government employees or make it impossible for such employees to find postgovernment positions. Public service, in short, should not imply a mandatory lifetime contract because the postemployment restrictions effectively prevent postgovernment employment. Although perfect fairness in this regard may be elusive, a one- or two-year "cooling-off period" between government service and the right to represent private individuals who seek government contracts or other benefits may be a fair approach to the problem.

One need look no further than the recent (1989) scandal at the Department of Housing and Urban Development (HUD)—involving allegations that the government was defrauded out of billions of dollars—to see what can happen when former, high-ranking officials have the unlimited right to visit former colleagues and subordinates on behalf of private sector clients.

Legal Standards for Ethical Behavior of Elected Officials

Laws requiring ethical behavior should also apply to those who are elected to public office. Legislation defining ethical behavior for elected officials is at least of equal importance and may be more important than legislation defining ethical standards for appointed officials.

There are two recurring themes that appear most frequently in laws that define the ethical standards of elected officials. First, particularly in units of local government, elected officials are not full-time employees. Thus the question arises as to when and under what circumstances part-time elected officials have a con-lict between their private sector positions and their elected responsibilities. The chair of the City Council Public Works Committee, for instance, should not be a local contractor or vendor who does business with the city and, of equal importance, should not represent such contractors or vendors. The conflict of interest problems are obvious.

But what about the part-time elected official whose responsibilities are acutely temporal or limited in some other way, such as the state senator who serves only for the first 90 days of each year while the state legislature is in session? Should a state senator who is a lawyer be prohibited from representing clients in lawsuits against the state? May the lawyer represent clients who have grievances with state administrative agencies or people who do business with the state?

The answers are (probably) that the lawyer/state senator should be prohibited from representing clients who wish to sue the state or have complaints against state agencies. There may be a different answer to the question of whether the lawyer can represent the businessperson who provides goods or services to the state. To some extent, the disclosure of the potential conflict will go a long way toward avoiding impropriety, but the question remains as to how disclosure should be made. The answer is obvious: through financial disclosure statements.

Such disclosure statements by elected officials should be required. Only if the public is informed about conflicts that may exist among elected public officials can the public feel confident that there are no such conflicts. As with other ethical imperatives, however, problems occur when such financial disclosures are required. For instance, should the part-time state senator/ lawyer be required to list for public inspection the identity of every client represented by the lawyer or the lawyer's law firm? If your answer to this question is in the affirmative, is your answer the same if the lawyer in question represents only clients accused of criminal tax violations or child abuse? Should a psychiatrist elected to a part-time legislative body be required to list for public inspection the names of his or her patients?

The problem with disclosing income from a law or medical practice without identifying the clients or patients who contributed to that income is that the potential conflict in question concerns the identity of clients or patients. The receipt of income is not by itself the potentially disqualifying factor.

At some point, disclosure statements that apply to elected officials will prevent some people from seeking election to public office. The question about the psychiatrist is not hypothetical; a state supreme court was forced to address this issue in a recent case and ruled that the state's financial disclosure laws applicable to elected officials required a state senator/psychiatrist to list all of his patients before the senator could assume office. It is hard to imagine, however, a conflict that might arise between the responsibilities of a mental health professional and the responsibilities of an elected official. It is less difficult to imagine a conflict between the responsibilities of a lawyer and the responsibilities of an elected official. If this is true, perhaps disclosure statements applicable to elected officials should be interpreted differently depending on the private sector responsibilities of such officials.

The second theme that appears frequently in laws applying to the ethics of elected officials concerns the extent to which such officials may accept gifts, services, honoraria, or contributions to political campaigns from institutions and people in the private sector. One commentator has stated that the scandals concerning these issues that have occurred in Washington, D.C., and numerous state capitols is not what is illegal but rather what is legal.[5] Free vacations, large fees for giving speeches, and substantial contributions during each campaign cycle are but a few of the things some elected officials are reported to have received.

Does the receipt of money influence elected officials? The speaker of one state assembly has commented, "If you can't drink their booze, eat their food, have their women, and vote against them in the morning, you don't belong in this place." Wholly apart from the graphic way the statement is made, its accuracy is questionable: On April 1, 1987, six members of the U.S. House of Representatives Armed Services Committee were paid $2,000 each just for coming to a breakfast sponsored by a company that manufactures trucks. A few hours later, an Armed Services subcommittee passed legislation that forced the army to purchase 500 trucks from the trucking company—a purchase the army did not want to make. When asked about the propriety of this, two of the representatives stated that it was merely a coincidence that the breakfast had occurred on the day of the vote.

Partially in response to recurring scandals, the U.S. Congress has considered legislation increasing the salaries of members of Congress but strictly limiting the right of members to receive honoraria or nonpolitical contributions. Presently, members of Congress are limited to outside income per year of $35,000 for senators and $26,000 for representatives. There is no limit for free vacations or noncash gifts. Members of Congress are paid $89,500 per year; the recommended legislation would raise the salary to $135,000—apparently in recognition of the ancient maxim that paying tigers more will not change their stripes, but it may attract a better class of tiger.

Although political contributions seem a necessary consequence of the democratic process, there should be some limits on the contributions an elected official can accept. It may be appropriate to base contributions on the kind of elected office that is being contested, with higher limits for national office (the House of Representatives, the Senate, the presidency). At present, $1,000 is the maximum amount a person or individual can donate to the political campaign of a person running for the U.S. Congress or the presidency. Political action committees can also donate funds to a campaign, as can other institutions. Although the reporting of contributions and limits on the amounts of contributions help maintain some semblance of propriety in the rough and tumble world of political fund raising, laws and regulations that enforce even more stringent ethical standards may be appropriate—as would more vigorous enforcement of existing laws and regulations.

Codes of Ethics

Several years ago, a colleague of ours served as deputy mayor of a large eastern city. During his first year of service, the mayor called our colleague to his office and, because the end of the year was approaching, asked our colleague to establish a policy concerning when and to what extent city employees could accept Christmas gifts from individuals and institutions that did business with the city. Being the careful and thoughtful person he is, our colleague decided to learn about the existing policy; he called to his office the heads of the city departments and inquired. "Well," they told him, "if you can eat it or drink it in one day, you can accept it as a Christmas gift. If you can't, it's too much."

Although microeconomists might applaud this ethical standard, our colleague did not. His rejection of it was hastened by further investigation revealing that during the previous Christmas, city employees were observed carrying to their cars turkeys, cases of liquor, and other food and drink in such quantity as to be incapable of consumption by even the largest of nuclear families in any period less than a week.

In response, our colleague established a new rule: any city employee who received any gift of any value from anyone, other than a relative by blood or marriage, would be summarily dismissed. In addition, those people and institutions that did business with the city were told that any person or organization that gave a gift of any value to any city employee at any time would be struck from the city's acceptable bidders list—forever—and that notice of such permanent debarment, in the event of violation, would be delivered by a uniformed police officer.

Without attempting to explain how our colleague's threatened actions meet even the minimum due process rights of public employees and those who do business with the government, we note that Christmas gifts were neither proffered to nor accepted by any city employee in that city during that Christmas season by anyone who directly or even indirectly did business with the city.

The city in which our colleague served did not have an ethical code for public employees. If it had, the question of when, if at all, a city employee could accept a Christmas gift from a person who did business with the city—or anyone else—might have been addressed. Ethical codes for public employees are hard to write, but they are an essential ingredient in maintaining the ethical conduct of such employees. By their very nature, ethical codes can describe appropriate conduct for situations that are not conducive to description in criminal codes. In addition, when the appropriate ethical conduct is not obvious due to the ambivalent nature of the situation, an ethical code can describe alternative choices. In short, ethical codes can describe what an employee must not do or must do, whereas criminal codes describe only prohibited conduct.

It might prove useful for the first draft of an employees' ethical code (or the amendments to an existing code) to be written by a committee of employees. In addition to the fact that an employee-written code will almost certainly be more acceptable to employees, experience has taught that at least some employee-drafted codes are far stricter than the employer would have dared to write. If such a code is to be written by an employee committee, it is essential that the committee include employees from different departments and levels of the government. Conduct that is ethical in one department may be found to be unethical in another.

At a minimum, an ethical code for government employees should include sections that describe to whom the code applies (full-time employees, part-time employees, consultants); preemployment conduct that eliminates an applicant from consideration as a public employee; a description of conduct that, though not of a criminal nature, is grounds for dismissal; conflicts of interest; postemployment restrictions; whether and to what extent the code is applicable to unethical conduct when there is no nexus between the conduct and government service (i.e., driving while intoxicated, participating in an adulterous relationship); and the extent to which the code mandates the reporting of unethical behavior observed in other government employees.

Public employee ethical codes should be mandatory reading at the time of employment. Although the importance of training is discussed in the next chapter, an ethical code that is neither read nor understood is useless or worse. So is an ethical code when compliance with it appears to be impossible.

Whether written by employees, independent consultants, a citizens group, or a combination of them, the code should be reasonable. Public employees can be held to higher standards of conduct than private-sector employees, but not unreasonably so. Maintaining ethical standards is important but will not be understood to be so if the public employees' ethical conduct describes a standard of conduct that is unattainable.

LAWS AND RULES: A CASE STUDY

The enactment of legislation, codes of ethics, or rules to increase government employees' sensitivity to ethical concerns must be coextensive with the ability of a government to function in an orderly and appropriate way. Laws or rules that increase ethical sensitivity but ignore their impact on government operations are almost always counterproductive.

Several years ago, in a midwest city, a scandal in the Buildings Department resulted in widespread reports of payoffs and bribes paid to city employees by building contractors who sought early, and sometimes impermissible, approval of building permits. As a result, procedures were altered (for the purpose of insuring ethical conduct) so that the original 5- or 6-step review process for the issuance of a building permit became a 25- to 35-step review process. It was the view of the authors of the new procedures that such multiple review and cross checking would decrease or even eliminate the opportunity for unethical behavior.

The authors were correct. There was an elimination of unethical conduct in the construction permit section of the Buildings Department. There was also an end to the issuance of building permits, and new construction virtually ground to a halt. The issuance of building permits was now such an unwieldly procedure that it was impossible to issue a construction permit. The ethical constraints made it impossible for the construction permit division to function.

A more recent and more interesting example of unquestionably important new ethics rules that interfere with the ability of the government to function is found in Public Law 100–679.[6] This section prohibits certain acts by government officials, employees, consultants and advisors, and those of competing contractors during the conduct of any federal agency procurement for property or services. For government officials and employees who have participated personally and substantially in the conduct of any federal agency procurement, there are additional restrictions on conduct for two years after the period of that involvement. The new section also covers certification and enforcement and sanctions such as administrative actions and contractual, civil, and criminal penalties.

The legislation was passed, in part, as a congressional response to the conviction of Michael Deaver, a former aide to President Reagan, as well as allegations of widespread corruption in federal procurement in the Department of Defense. The latter allegations included accusations of "side switching"—former Department of Defense officials employed by defense contractors and thereafter receiving from former employees, including subordinates, hundreds of millions of dollars in government contracts—and the payment of bribes to Department of Defense procurement officials.

The new act requires appropriate governmentwide regulations and guidelines to be issued by the Federal Acquisition Regulation (FAR) within 180 days of enactment. The act, which was passed in October 1988 without any hearings and with practically no debate in Congress, restricts government personnel with respect to postemployment, seeking employment, gratuities, and disclosure of information. The regulations implementing the act, however, were so complicated and created such controversy that on May 15, 1989, Congress passed S.968, which delayed implementation of the act (from 180 days after passage) until July 16, 1989.[7]

Fewer than 90 days after implementation, the *Washington Post* reported that Pentagon officials who met with Defense contractors had to read a number of legal questions from a printed card similar to a card police officers use when reading "Miranda" warnings to suspects arrested for the commission of a crime. The questions are intended to determine if the conversation is legally permissible.

The incentive for unethical behavior is at its highest during procurement activities, as noted in Chapter 3. It is almost impossible, therefore, to criticize legislation and regulations that are intended to insure ethical conduct by procurement officials. But when the legislation results in uncertainty as to scope and intent, and when Miranda warnings must be read before procurement negotiations can continue, the wisdom of the legislation must be questioned.

In addition, neither the legislation in question nor the regulations are a model of clarity. It is unclear, for instance, whether the act permits an individual to recuse himself or herself from a procurement in order to engage in employment discussions with a *competing* contractor. It is also unclear whether a government employee who participated personally and substantially in a procurement that results in a contract award can enter into employment discussions with the contractor while a modification to the contract is being negotiated.

Clarity and knowledge of the precise language of an act or regulations is not merely an academic issue. On June 27, 1989, the United States Court of Appeals for the District of Columbia Circuit reversed the conviction of Franklin (Lyn) Nofziger, assistant to the president (Reagan) for political affairs, on the grounds that Nofziger did not "know" that certain communications he made to officials of the White House after he returned to private employment were in violation of a criminal statute prohibiting certain communications for one year after government employment has ceased.[8]

In its opinion, the Court of Appeals summarized the issue as follows:

The parties agree that an ex-official may lawfully lobby his former agency the day after he has left it with the purpose of *stimulating* its interest in a matter of importance to a private client *so long as* that matter is not already before the agency and the agency does not already have a direct and substantial interest in it. If, however, the agency should already have such an interest, the government contends that what would otherwise have been an entirely innocent communication is transformed into a felony punishable by two years in jail *even though* the former official had no knowledge of the fact. Thus, the government's interpretation would impose strict criminal liability on a lobbyist (by definition, one who communicates with the intent to influence) who is misinformed as to what matters are of current interest to his former employer. Nofziger, on the other hand, maintains that a former employee cannot be found in violation of subsection 207(c) unless it can be shown that he had knowledge that the agency had a "direct and substantial" interest in the matter.

The question of whether a former government employee is in violation of a criminal statute should not be judged on such legal numbras and pennumbras as these. Clarity, brevity, and the ability to coexist with government operations is a predicate for legislation and regulations intended to encourage ethical behavior.

NOTES

1. See, for example, Florida Statutes, Sections 286.011.

2. The federal government has both conflict of interest rules. The criminal statute is 18 U.S.C Sections 201–9. The broader standards are found in Executive Order 11222, which was issued by President Lyndon Johnson in 1965. The U.S. Civil Service Commission has drafted regulations that are based on the Executive Order and that must be used as a model for each federal government department's ethics rules. These regulations are found at 5 Code of Federal Regulations, Part 735.

3. *Peters, et al. v. Ashland Oil.*

4. "Open-Door Policy, Closed-Door Practice," *Washington Post*, November 14, 1989.

5. George Will, "The Ethics of Politics," *Newsweek*, September 9, 1989.

6. The public law amends the Office of Federal Procurement Policy Act (41 U.S.C. 401–20) by adding a new Section 27, entitled "Procurement Integrity."

7. In addition, numerous amendments and corrections to the regulations were published (54 Fed. Reg. 12556, 21066 and 22282).

8. 18 U.S.C. § 207(c).

7

Four Essentials of the Ethical Practice of Government

An enthusiastic music lover from a rural town went to New York City for the first time to attend a recital at Carnegie Hall. Getting off the bus, he headed uptown and became lost. He spotted a man carrying a violin case, stopped him, and said, "Excuse me. Can you tell me how to get to Carnegie Hall?" The man replied, "Practice, practice, practice!" The ethical behavior of government employees requires the same perseverance in the establishment and maintenance of systematic management practices to support its preventive and proactive elements and substantially reduce the reactive mode. These four essentials are training, audit of management, investigation, and management control. For these essentials to be performed at a virtuoso level, they must be proactively nurtured in a positive organizational and management culture.

ORGANIZATIONAL AND MANAGEMENT CULTURE

Ethical behavior always is relative to a culture. It reflects consensus on acceptable standards of conduct, social obligations, and duties. Ethical behavior also is relative to an era. In fact, one could say it's situational. We make ethical decisions within the confines of a given situation or sets of similar situations.

What we decide to do is governed to a great extent by what we have learned and experienced.

Our way of life is transmitted from one generation to another by learning and experience. Cultural universals such as religion, social and economic organization, and political structure all impact our lives. Through a conscious and unconscious process, we filter a never-ending flood of information and experience, all shaped by these universals. The universals inherently are neutral. Few would argue against "a democratic form of government," for example. We make value judgments based on what we allow through the filter and behave accordingly. In the unique democracy of the United States, public officials must understand their leadership role in fostering the highest standards of ethical government practice. An ethical organizational and management culture begins with strong principled leadership, credibility, and visibility.

The framers of the U.S. Constitution believed that government and its workers should be ethical. The Founding Fathers incorporated much of John Calvin's attempt to establish a theocracy in Geneva in establishing the republic. Calvin, a strong believer in original sin, believed that government should be structured to take into account the total depravity of people and to lift them to higher standards of behavior. The U.S. system of checks and balances among the three branches of government was an attempt to incorporate these higher standards as a counterbalance to humankind's tendency for less than ethical behavior. All of the great documents make reference to the Deity and, by inference, to moral behavior. The closing paragraph in the Declaration contains these two references: "appealing to the Supreme Judge of the World, in the rectitude of our intentions" and "with a firm reliance on the Protection of Divine Providence." The Constitution makes provision for removal of the president and vice-president from office by impeachment and all civil officers on impeachment for and conviction of treason, bribery, or other high crimes and misdemeanors. Many state mottoes make reference to the Deity. Government employees, therefore, are expected to adhere to a higher standard of ethical behavior than might be expected in the private sector.

The concept of professionals as administrators of public services was based on a strong sense of morality and a reaction to political machines that believed in the spoils systems. The political machines were installed early in America. Aaron Burr and his involvement with Tammany Hall institutionalized political control of public office at all levels in the East and served as the prototype for similar organizations in cities and counties as the nation expanded West. Statements such as Tammany Sachem Plunkett's "honest graft" to the late New Jersey political boss Frank Hague's "I am the law" typified a morality machined to tolerances dictated by the American tradition of the inseparability of politics, control of funds for the administration of public programs, insider information on major real estate and construction programs, and similar funneling of public funds into private pockets. After all, to the victor belongs the spoils.

Historically, the spoils system reflected the practice of rewarding loyal party members with appointments to federal posts such as local postmasters and jobs in the federal government executive branch, foreign embassies, and consulates. Our earliest presidents, notably Thomas Jefferson, adopted this practice, which became widespread during the administration of Andrew Jackson. The resultant corruption and inefficiencies of this political patronage process became too much under President Ulysses S. Grant and led to the creation of the Civil Service Commission in 1871. Its successor, the Office of Personnel Management (OPM), has little control over the spoils system, which continues today for a substantial number of federal, state, and local office appointees. Reauthorization of the Office of Government Ethics in 1988 moved the Office out of the OPM into a separate executive agency. In its current configuration it suffers from its antecedent in being woefully underfunded and dependent on other federal agencies for many of its mandated functions.

Survival of the spoils system is not limited to the federal government's and the 50 states' office appointees. We also are talking about some 65,000 municipal managers and some 18,500 county officials, the overwhelming majority of whom are appointees. We also are talking about 3,000 counties, 17,000 cities, more than 40,000 school districts, and close to 10,000 other agencies and jurisdictions—park, sanitary, fire protection, and sewer districts—who make decisions that affect the quality of our lives and the expenditure of our dollars. Bill and Nancy Boyarsky, in *Backroom Politics,* concluded that "for the most part, our worst suspicions were confirmed: State and local governments are run with almost total disregard for the average voter. We found countless examples showing how the system of backroom politics works."[1] The Boyarskys documented numerous unethical practices, ranging from secret business campaign contributions to unpublicized meetings between land developers and county executives to bypass limits on sewer capacity to control of thousands of patronage jobs in our major cities. No level of government is missed, from former President Richard Nixon and Vice-President Spiro Agnew to former Mayor Richard Daley and assorted county supervisors and city officials. Backroom politics reek with the smoke of unsavory, unethical deals. When Energy Secretary James D. Watkins joined the Bush Cabinet in 1989, he stated that he was not at all pleased by what he found in his first few months in office. He reported that the Department of Energy culture had to be changed. Among the problems he reported at a press conference in June of 1989 were:

- Incompatability between nuclear plant operating philosophy and a healthy, safe environment
- Insufficient scientific information
- Sloppy contracts with civilian plant managers
- Lack of trained personnel

An ethical organizational and management culture should be uncompromising on those universals that reflect the best in all of us. It should reflect those fundamental characteristics that can withstand the fads and expediencies that seem appropriate in a given situation but that represents compromise on our ideals, standards, and ethics. The culture should reject what in our "heart of hearts" we know is unethical and immoral. It should reflect the real test of a person's belief system and resulting ethical behavior—what that person would do if assured that no one would ever check up or find out what was done or left undone.

The culture we should foster is one in which we pay attention to our conscience and make those choices between moral right and wrong as they affect our motives and behavior. "Let your conscience be your guide," as is true of many cliches, is well founded in experience. Public service carries with it the obligation to do what is right or not to do what is wrong. A conscience is not part of the double helix of the inherited characteristics of our chromosomes. It is delicate and must be nurtured, protected, and defended against environmental hazards. The old-fashioned attributes of integrity and honesty are another aspect of the culture in which government should operate. An honest government, perceived that way by the public, represents the ideal of the Founding Fathers. It fosters confidence that public resources are being spent to accomplish the most good for the most people. An honest government precludes the kind of unethical practices detailed in this and other chapters in our book.

The Preamble to the Constitution of the United States of America includes the phrase "promote the general welfare." This universal element of public service reflects the belief that the general welfare of society is an essential goal of those who are delegated the public trust. It is promotion of the general welfare that public employees must address, not the welfare of a few to the detriment of the many.

We hear a lot about "role models" in many walks of life. Some professional athletes are included in public-service television spots endorsing various community-service programs or urging young people to "say no to drugs." Media stars promote commercial products. Former astronauts also pitch certain products. Ad agencies learned a long time ago that celebrities, people of influence, real or perceived role models, move products. The same is true of government leaders. The flagship product they are moving is ethical government practice. They have an obligation to serve as the ethical role model for those who look to them for leadership.

White Sneakers and Brown Socks

The district attorney in New York City learned about possible unethical practices in the candidate-examination process for appointment as a police officer. Thousands of applicants took the exam each year for a small percentage of appointments. The test was the critical first step in the process. Investigation determined that one person was "guaranteeing" a passing score on the exam if the candidates did precisely what they were told. First, they paid the guarantor $100 in cash. Second, they were told to wear white sneakers and brown socks to the examination. According to witnesses, the candidates were told that the exam proctors were in on the deal and would make sure their papers were handled appropriately. After weeks of wiretapping, investigators sitting in and taking the examination, tailing the proctors, and interviewing the wearers of white sneakers and brown socks, the New York City District Attorney's Office concluded that the exam dress code was a scam. There was no proven link between the person who collected the $100 and any New York City Police Department employee. In fact, wiretaps showed that some candidates tracked down the person running the scam and complained about failing the exam after payment of the $100. "Hey, no problem," the scam artist replied in each case. "There are thousands of people who take the exam, and every once in a while, the proctors screw up. Let's meet and I'll return your $100."

This scam demonstrates the continuing gullibility and the attempt on the part of a segment of the public to get a little more of the edge in any way possible on getting what they want. It also demonstrates the perception on the part of the police officer candidates that the culture of the New York City Police Department selection process was open to unethical practices. Whether or not this perception was based on truth is irrelevant. People behave on their perception of a given situation. They may or may not have the facts or have what they believe are the facts. It is their perception of the real or false information that will determine behavior.

We have had many examples of people buying into a culture of lies, half-truths, and misinformation these past 50 years. Wisconsin Senator Joseph McCarthy (1947–1957) conducted an aggressive campaign against people in high office that he termed *traitors* and *Communists* that was shown to be unsubstantiated. His colleagues in the U.S. Senate condemned him for his behavior in

1954, after which his influence declined. President Reagan's first budget director, David Stockman, convinced him and the Congress that the president's budget and fiscal policies were solidly arrived at and that the administration's legislative program should be enacted with dispatch. It was enacted in almost all essential elements. When Stockman left the Office of Management and Budget, he disclosed that much of what was presented to Congress in those early days of Reagan's incumbency was not that solidly derived. The 1982 Reagan budget, for example, included a bookkeeping invention described by Stockman as the "magic asterisk," or "future savings to be identified."[2] Stockman telegraphed the Reagan administration's strategy in 1981 when he adopted Senator Howard Baker's prestidigitatorial punctuation phrase. The "additional budget reductions to be announced by the President at a later date would allow everyone to finesse the hard questions for now."[3] The hard questions continued to be finessed through Reagan's reelection and the Bush administration. Neither the executive nor legislative branches of government have been willing to address the "magic asterisk" as the sleight-of-hand it is for fear of alienating the electorate and upsetting the culture of apathy about our declining national fiscal health. President Bush's first budget director, Richard G. Darman, has followed the pattern established by Stockman under Reagan by "a business-as-usual attitude toward fiscal gimmickry. The economic assumptions underlying it, which include a combination of robust economic growth and sharply declining interest rates, are absurdly optimistic."[4] The public message by Bush on increasing spending with no tax increases was not reflected in his first printed budget submission to Congress. At that time, House Budget Committee chairman Leon A. Panetta (D-Calif.) charged that members of the Bush administration "basically want to play the same games we've played the last eight years."[5] Again, it is the people's perception of the situation in the organizational culture that will determine their behavior.

The Actual and the Appearance

An ethical organizational culture is built on observable practices. It also depends on perceptions about the practices, or how they look to those inside and outside government. Public officials cannot avoid continuous employee and public scrutiny on what they say and do. Since neither of these two "publics" are privy to everything that occurs in the conduct of government, they rely on a variety of media to form perceptions about how things are going and the degree to which they appear to be going well. Government employees are part of the organizational culture and receive numerous written materials that inform them and direct them in matters of general and specific importance to their jobs. A culture in which ethical practices periodically are addressed incorporates both action and appearance to reinforce preventive and maintenance behaviors consistent with that jurisdiction's ethos.

For example, the August 1986 booklet *Practical Ethics for Chiefs of Mission and All Department of State and Foreign Service Employees* states: "Our laws, our regulations, indeed, our values forbid not only the breach of ethical standards, but even the appearance of such a breach. We have prepared this briefing book on practical ethics to assist you and you staff to recognize and deal with situations which may *result in* or *create the appearance* of (unethical practices)."[6]

The booklet contains six sections with specific laws and regulations that govern the activity described at the end of each section. Each section deals with situations that may result in or create the appearance of unethical acts. The section headings are "Confidence of the Public in the Integrity of the U.S. Government"; "Impeding Government Efficiency or Economy"; "Using Public Office for Private Gain"; "Losing Independence or Impartiality of Action"; "Making Government Decisions Outside Official Channels"; and "Giving Preferential Treatment to Any Organization or Person."[7]

Like those in all federal Inspector General Offices, this booklet is supplemented by semiannual reports to the Congress that detail department audits, inspections, investigations, and compliance with recommendations to prevent unethical practices and improve management in prevention and maintenance of an ethical organizational culture.

Appearance . . . and More

In 1984 Edwin Meese III asked for a special prosecutor to investigate his personal financial dealings. At the time, Meese was counselor to President Reagan. The special prosecutor found no basis for prosecution on any of some 11 allegations including, for example, whether Meese had arranged federal jobs for people who helped him financially. The special prosecutor said his jurisdiction did not permit him to judge Meese on the ethics. Meese, then the nominee for attorney general of the United States, claimed the trouble was not of his creation but of others distorting his activities.

In 1987 Attorney General Meese again asked for a special prosecutor to investigate his personal, financial, and official relationships concerning a minority-owned tool-and-die maker in the Bronx called Wedtech. Several friends and associates of Meese and a former White House aide, Lyn C. Nofziger, were doing work for Wedtech. They also included the attorney general's lawyer, E. Robert Wallach. The *New York Times* reported involvement of other associates of Meese with Wedtech and an investment-limited blind partnership of which Meese was a partner.[8] State and federal investigations into Wedtech began in the fall of 1986. Meese did not disqualify himself from Justice Department inquiries into Wedtech until the middle of 1987.

In his 1988 report, the independent counsel decided not to indict Meese on any of the charges that were the subject of his extensive investigation. He did state that he believed Meese had broken the law in two instances and that he could prove it in court. The independent counsel decided not to prosecute because he didn't think an average citizen would have been prosecuted for the same illegal practices. No evidence surfaced that Meese intended to break the law. Meese replied to the findings of the independent counsel by attacking him for violating every principle of fairness and decency.

In January 1989 an internal Justice Department report on former Attorney General Edwin Meese concluded that he engaged in "conduct which should not be tolerated of any government employee, especially not the attorney general" and that disciplinary action by the president would be warranted if Meese were still the nation's number one law enforcement officer. The report, issued by the Justice Department's Office of Professional Responsibility, found that the former attorney general committed numerous violations of departmental regulations and the 1965 executive order setting out ethical standards for government employees. In response to Meese's public statements about not being indicted as a result of the independence counsel's report, the Office of Professional Responsibility reported that:

Based upon the foregoing, we have concluded that Mr. Meese violated both the Executive Order and the Department's Standards of Conduct. It is axiomatic that such violations are inconsistent with the ethical obligations of the Attorney General of the United States. The Executive Order mandates that when a set of circumstances is presented which could involve a government official in a situation giving rise to an appearance of impropriety, he takes affirmative action to avoid that situation. For the Attorney General in particular we view the Executive Order setting forth his minimum ethical requirements. Indeed, former Attorney General William French Smith recognized the appropriate standard for Attorneys General when he declared (on May 28, 1982) that an Attorney General must take action to remedy even an inaccurate appearance of impropriety. The American public is entitled to both the appearance and reality of impartial, honest government. If the public perceives that something is amiss in the Department of Justice, then, for all practical purposes, something is amiss. Whether the perception is an accurate one is not the point, because the loss of confidence in the institution is the same. All Department employees should be required to ensure that their conduct does not contribute to such a perception.[9]

We trust that this analysis will lay to rest the claims by Meese that the appropriate standard for official behavior is whether an independent counsel seeks an official's indictment. We found that the independent counsel's report far from vindicates Meese; rather, it details conduct that should not be tolerated of any government employee, especially not the attorney general of the United States. Were he still serving as attorney general, we would recommend to the acting attorney general that the president take disciplinary action.[10]

Meese's own deputy attorney general, Arnold Burns, testified in Congress that according to Meese everybody was wrong, willfully or otherwise. Arnold Burns likened life in the Justice Department to Alice in Wonderland's world. He stated that Meese still "clings to the thought that he committed no crime ... no wrong ... no act of impropriety ... no ethical violation ... nor error of good taste or bad judgement," and "if he had to do it over again he would comport himself in the same way."[11] The ethical issue here is Mr. Meese's inability or refusal to see or understand the perception that others have of what was wrong in his dealings with Wedtech, Wallach, and other matters involving income tax reporting and a proposed Iraqi oil pipeline. Meese's "Response to the Report of the Office of Professional Responsibility," in January 1989, submitted on his behalf by his legal counsel, asserts that there is absolutely no basis for criticism and terms the report unprofessional, without legal basis, grossly distorted and ignoring of the facts, without legitimate foundation, and wrong on certain specific matters. His counsel concludes that:

OPR's treatment of former Attorney General Meese is a travesty of Justice. OPR has purposely attempted to degrade Mr. Meese's reputation without providing him even the most basic rudiments of fair play. It has ignored the facts, the law, decency and common sense both in the process it has used and in the conclusion it reaches.[12]

President-Elect George Bush apparently learned some lessons from the Reagan transition-team operations. According to a 1982 GAO study, most agencies did not have information on what transition-team members' business interests were.[13] The GAO found no evidence of transition-team members using their access to inside documents for their own personal benefit. In addition to compliance with the 1988 Presidential Transitions Effectiveness Act, however, which requires such disclosure of names, salaries, and business affiliations of all transition-team members, Bush required a strict ethics pledge from every transition-team member. This action by Bush clearly established the moral high ground and conveyed a clear, unequivocal message about the ethical behavior expected from anyone involved in the transition process. This was followed by appointment of an ethics commission to draft clear and unequivocal guidelines concerning ethical behavior of federal government employees at all levels.

Then there is the cultural universal of morality—the distinction between right and wrong. Sometimes, *ethics* and *morality* are used synonymously. Ethics relates more to human conduct, morality more to the principles underlying ethical behavior. Morality has to do with what people think is correct, right, or necessary. The ever-present danger for all of us is that morals and ethics can be distorted by demagogues and scoundrels clothed in respectability. What is considered "normal" or deriving a "consensus" about what is acceptable practice from one element of the culture to the detriment of the others can be disastrous. Entire cultures can go along with what is immoral and unethical. In the United States, for example, "separate and equal facilities" was the law until the 1950s. Residents of Shelby County (Tenn.) and Hudson County (N.J.) accepted Bosses Crump's and Hague's de facto standards of morality. The horror of the Holocaust occurred because the moral consensus of Germany, Austria, Poland, and other European countries accepted and supported what Hitler was selling—the destruction of 6 million Jews. Iran's Ayatollah Khomeini publicly ordered the execution of an author in another country because he believed the author was blasphemous and fanned Moslems into a religious frenzy. The resignation of House Speaker Jim Wright in May 1989 resulted from a combination of a changing ethical paradigm of the "ground rules" on what was acceptable in getting around House standards on outside income and Republican anger at the treatment of John Tower, President Bush's nominee for secretary of defense.

The organizational and managerial culture must reflect these attributes and values and recognize that they inherently go along with public service in our democracy. Leaders, too, must accept and reflect these values.

A career of administrative statesmanship must consist of more than the trite discussion of "moral dilemmas"—whistleblowing, wire-tapping— it must center on the balance of virtues which public officials in different positions in government must display. Those virtues are rather obvious: a respect for the law, a concept of the public interest, courage, tenacity, and prudence, to name a few.[14]

The personal example of the top manager or administrator— department, agency, jurisdiction—is itself a cultural universal that conveys a very clear message to all those in the government unit concerned. The message can reinforce the ethical practice of government or contribute to its erosion. The cultural environment created by government leaders at any level can enhance or diminish:

the desire to be respected by the public, so that being a politician or civil servant can be considered an honorable career, and election, appointment or employment in government can be considered evidence of high personal standards of conduct. Recognition that corruption has a high social as well as monetary cost, and that even though the public may not seem to care in situations where corruption exists, and may continue to vote-in administrations that are either too dirty or stupid to be believed, the social cost is still being paid. When corruption and the costs of corruption become unacceptable, the result is likely to be personal as well as civic peril.

The awareness that there are standards of morality and ethical conduct that can be agreed on, and principles of ethical action that can be applied, so that an employee or official can have confidence that he/she is acting morally and ethically and need not be at the mercy of a superior's whim or an investigative reporter's slow news day.[15]

In one city, a young programmer on the night shift programmed the city computer to cast horoscopes. They became quite popular and a daily practice among many employees. The city manager learned about it from his administrative assistant who asked her if she wanted hers done. The city manager called the director of finance.

Fred, I'm assuming you didn't know this was going on and that it started in your department. Frankly, that's a partial copout for me and not that flattering for you. However, the computer is the city's, paid for by taxpayers, and these horoscopes cost time and money. It stops now. Suspend the young man for as long as it takes at his daily rate until he pays back what it cost us for the time it took for the horoscope program. Then, figure out how much it cost the city for each and every one of those horoscopes. Send me a list of every one who got one because I am going to send them a bill. Look, . . . I don't even use the office Xerox for personal stuff—it's not right.[16]

The city manager demonstrated strong, principled leadership that is hostile to unethical practices. Casting horoscopes on the city's time and using the city computer were wrong. The city manager's follow-up to her employees corrected the problem and reinforced the expected ethical standard.

One of the more curious aspects of recent American politics was the "Teflon" quality of President Reagan in relation to the numerous indictments and convictions of his closest aides for unethical practices. Repeatedly, the president defended his aides and publicly decried their convictions. Apparently, little or no concern existed about the perception of the public and those appointed by Reagan and the cultural climate created and fostered. The president publicly demonstrated unflagging loyalty for his former appointees. He may best have summed up his attitude when he responded to public concerns about the influence peddling of his former deputy chief of staff, Michael Deaver. People are complaining about him, the president said, because he's been darned successful and deservedly so. Reagan, while still in office, also accepted a $2.5 million house on 1.25 acres of land in Bel Air, California, paid for by 18 "investors" who started collecting "rent" when he left office. Only two of the 18 were identified,

although a number of the investors had served as advisors to the President. . . . But for all of this, Ronald Reagan the beneficiary, was basically spared any criticism by political adversary, the press or the public. He was, in fact, so boyishly innocent that you couldn't imagine him having a corrupt bone in his body. (That was why his sale of arms to the terrorist ayatollah upset and disillusioned millions.) Because he was the Last Innocent Man, people somehow did not believe Ronald Reagan would be seduced, or even influenced, by a house in Bel Air. . . . And unlike most politicians, Ronald Reagan seemed to live in a magnetic field where troubles miraculously flowed away from him.[17]

Compare this to those members of Congress who, for trying to win themselves a pay raise to cover the high cost of running households in both Washington and their home states, have been catching it daily in the press. The House leader or chairman who accepted the kindness of 16 unnamed "independently wealthy" benefactors would be committing political suicide. It is more than double standards; it's tough standards and no standards.[18]

Nancy Reagan, too, contributed to the breach of ethics by breaking her promise in 1982 to report gifts and loans on the Reagan's financial statements: "She broke her word. Some of the gowns (loaned her) were worth an estimated $15,000—about as much as a car—and the loan of them needed to be disclosed, the White House Counsel told Mrs. Reagan in 1982."[19]

Representative Patricia Schroeder's "Index of Clippings of Alleged Ethics Violations and Other Improprieties by Reagan Administration Appointees" further underlines the paradox of the reality of the Reagan administration's organizational culture of unethical conduct by hundreds of appointees and officeholders and the public's perception of a "squeaky clean" president.[20]

An ethical organizational and management culture reflects the belief that social goals and social responsibilities always outweigh one's personal gain. In an organizational context, legality alone cannot determine what is ethical. Laws can be perverted as the Nuremberg trials demonstrated. Laws without ethics remove the person from the cultural elements of morality and integrity. When ethics and public law or policy collide, the individual has to make decisions. The dilemmas for public employees surface when what is legal may be unethical. This confluence of cultural universalities is where strong and principled leadership makes the critical difference in favor of ethical behavior. Without an ethical organizational and management culture that encourages and fosters personal decisions about right and wrong, without diligent practice, the public sector will not make it to Carnegie Hall.

TRAINING

The public and private sectors spend millions of dollars each year on a wide range of training, for all levels of employees, everything from sophisticated technical skills to management practices fostering human-resources development. In addition, almost all government agencies provide some kind of orientation for new employees about the agency and how things get done. Many agencies also hand out material that includes a "Code of Ethics" and, on occasion, reprints of various laws, codes, administrative policies, and procedures that address what an employee may or may not do to function within the law. With few exceptions, these materials are not discussed and translated into practical examples of the kind of ethical dilemmas they may face in their jobs. But employees are expected to read the material, which is often complicated legalese, and apply what they may have read to the range of dilemmas they certainly will face during a day's or week's work.

The Office of Government Ethics (OGE) program for training incoming federal employees is typical of these *de minibus* attempts. The OGE sends letters to federal agencies offering to assist them in their ethics training programs, including those for new hires. The OGE publishes and sells a pamphlet, "How to Keep Out of Trouble," for use by federal agencies. In 1987 the OGE produced a videotape, *How to Complete the Executive Personnel Financial Disclosure Report*, and, the following year, another videotape, *Public Service, Public Trust*. This latter videotape, available by purchase, reviews conflict of interest laws and regulations applicable to executive branch employees.[21] Given the inadequate funding levels for the OGE, this clearly is not an aggressive training effort on ethics for executive-branch leadership.

Training is a key element in making sure that from the beginning all new employees—appointed, career, and elected, at all levels—know and understand the organization's ethical stance, the special nature of public service, and the personal obligations that are inherent in accepting and maintaining the public trust. Executive Order Number 1122, "Standards of Ethical Conduct for Government Officers and Employees," Part 1, Section 101, succinctly summarizes the standard for federal employees: "Where government is based on the consent of the governed, every citizen is entitled to have complete confidence in the integrity of his government. Each individual officer, employee, or adviser of government must help to earn and must honor that trust by his own integrity and conduct in all official actions. This standard is applicable at any level of government."[22]

The reasons for current and subsequent unethical practices by government officers, employees, and advisers substantially can be reduced by a well-designed training program that sensitizes employees to the accepted standard for ethical conduct; provides them with experience-based, pragmatic examples of pitfalls to avoid; and requires refresher training on a regular basis on changes in policy and procedures relating to standards of conduct and specific problems identified and resolved. Although there are some generic, governmentwide ethical problems that should be incorporated into every orientation and training program, the emphasis should be agency-specific. These efforts should be designed to share specific, identified problems in management controls, audits, and investigations, as well as case studies or dilemmas the agency has faced and employees probably will face at some time. Employees also should be viewed from the perspective of how they arrived in office—whether they were elected, appointed, or are in career positions. There are historical differences in the kinds of ethical dilemmas that "come with the territory," depending on the kind of government official concerned. Elected officials are more vulnerable to unethical campaign practices and peddlers of influence. Appointed officials are more vulnerable to influencing contracts in favor of party loyalists. Career officials are more vulnerable to postemployment deals that favor future employers. Therefore, training for these different groups should factor in these areas of special vulnerability and emphasize both the pitfalls and how they can be avoided.

The "Standards of Conduct Course" for the National Aeronautics and Space Administration (NASA) Goddard Space Flight Center employees (1988) and the companion *Standards of Conduct for NASA Employees* handbook (1987) represent a standard compilation of relevant statutes and regulations governing employees ethical practices. Of particular value in the course material is "Part 5. Case Studies." Ten case studies are presented that cover dilemmas ranging from outside employment to acceptance of gifts and from spousal conflict of interest to the competitive procurement process, as well as others specific to NASA/Goddard's situation. Following the ten case studies, "Part 6. Case Study Solutions" documents the appropriate resolution of the dilemmas and cites the relevant statutes and regulations for each. Case Study 1, for example, concerns an offer of transportation.

Norman is an engineer assigned to the staff of a flight project. The project has an ongoing contract with a company located in California, under which a spacecraft is being fabricated. As part of a trip to attend a semi-annual contract review meeting at the contractor's plant, Norman has approval to attend an IEEE conference in Arizona on the way there. Before leaving, he learns that some of the employees of the contractor will be attending the conference and have arranged for a company airplane to transport them back to California. There is plenty of room on the plane and Norman is invited to take advantage of the transportation. What should he do?[23]

The solution for this case study dilemma addresses the role of a government employee in relation to a government contractor and states that:

Norman should decline the invitation and refuse the transportation. The transportation is being offered by a company which has a contractual relationship with NASA. Acceptance is prohibited by 5 CFR 735.202(a) and (f) and by NHB 1900.1. Paragraph 202 (none of the exceptions in para. 202(d) apply automatically). Note that para. 202(d) authorizes acceptance of such interstate transportation if prior approval is granted by the Associate Administrator for Management.[24]

Employees of the Connecticut Department of Administrative Services prepared ethics questions for the executive director and general counsel of the state's Ethics Commission for use in training sessions. They included:

1. Is it a conflict of interest to hold a professional license and make use of it on the outside?

2. Another state agency would like to use you as a consultant; does this conflict with the ethics code? If so, are there any exceptions?

3. What should you do when you perceive a conflict of interest between your job and the vendor or company you may have to deal with? For example, you own stock in Company A and are involved in the purchasing of computer hardware and software.

4. What do you do if a vendor asks to pick up transportation costs for a meeting at its site?

5. A relative of yours is asked to consult for another state agency; is that a violation of ethical conduct? If so, by whom . . . you or your relative?

6. Is it permissible to accept holiday gifts from a vendor? For example, bottles of wine at Christmas?

7. What is the definition of "lobbyist" for the ethics code? How broad is this?[25]

This method of providing agency-specific examples and their solutions accomplishes three major training purposes: (1) the dilemmas are moved from the academic, general level to the real world; (2) the solutions cite relevant statutes and regulations as they have been applied, providing employees with a yardstick to use in the future; and (3) the case studies reinforce the agency's commitment to integrity and trust as the ethical standard for all employees.

The purpose of training as an essential strategy is not to provide every employee with an answer to every conceivable ethical problem that may occur. Even if that were possible, emerging technologies, new statutes and regulations, changing social mores, and the range of human behavior would not provide ready-made solutions for new situations. The growing numbers of women in the workplace, for example, have surfaced a number of public-service ethical dilemmas concerning possible spousal conflicts of interest. Consider a situation in which one married partner runs the family business and the other works for an agency department in a procurement decision position. The family business seeks contracts for the goods or services being sought by that agency department, creating a potential ethical dilemma. Then, too, an expanding female work force and the equal rights movement have led to increased protections for women against gender discrimination and sexual harassment, problems that were present and kept quiet until recently.

All Levels of Employees Need Training

A former city manager was called one day and asked to come to the city's major maintenance plant. He was told that he would enjoy "the surprise" the men who worked there had for him. When he arrived, he was shown a small airplane a number of city maintenance men had made. The city manager asked a number of questions and determined that the plane was built on city time, using city materials, and with the approval of the men's supervisor and plant manager. The supervisor told the city manager that the men "only worked on down time, when they didn't have anything special to do." The city manager brought action against the supervisor and manager that resulted in termination of their employment. The men who built the plane were reprimanded and deductions taken from their salaries until the estimated cost of the improperly used materials was recovered. Although the manager and supervisor did not participate in the construction of the airplane, they knew it was being built and did nothing.

What this case illustrates is that ethics training for all levels of the work force is necessary to insure that everyone starts with or has reinforced the same principles, understandings, and resources to assist in responding to any ethical dilemmas they may face. The design of training is critical in addressing the needs of different levels of employees, their length of service, and the specific responsibilities of their jobs. Distributing codes of ethics, posting them on the office wall, handing out pamphlets on standards of conduct, and even reviewing statutes and regulations in orientation sessions or brief review meetings represent the minimum that can be done. The results also will be minimum if this is all that is done. Information alone carries no guarantee that appropriate behavior will follow. The media daily report that lawyers and judges, among the most literate and articulate of professionals, are being indicted and convicted of unethical and illegal acts. What is needed is the translation of the information and ethical standards into behavior that honors public trust.

What All Public Employees Need to Know

The ethical practice of government requires that a core of information and generic problem areas with appropriate solutions to them be provided to all public employees. Generally, jurisdictions that require this core training incorporate it in orientation sessions for new employees. On occasion, usually after a rash of unethical or illegal acts on the part of members of a particular government administration, a flurry of special training and other well-publicized actions will be announced and held. As soon as the media move to other, "late breaking news" the ethics training is shelved. Inclusion of a solid core on ethical practice of government is critical in helping new employees begin public service with the understanding and confidence that will support their decisions in the public interest.

Review of ethics and staff-conduct training programs conducted by a number of federal and local jurisdictions and those we have conducted have led to this recommended generic content for new employee orientation and training:

- A clear and concise statement by the jurisdiction or agency head on expectations concerning the ethical behavior of all employees.[26]

- The statutes, ordinances, formal code of ethics, regulations, rules, and procedures within which they must operate and penalties for not observing them.

- The organization's management philosophy and rules, how they are enforced, safeguards against groundless accusations or unfairness, how disciplinary codes are enforced, and appeals procedures.

- What constitutes ethical practice in government and what are the dilemmas most commonly faced by employees of this jurisdiction and, specifically, by this agency. Included under this area would be: conflicts of interest, negotiations for outside employment and postemployment activities, gifts and favors, information that may or may not be disclosed, political activity, whistleblowing, and resources available to discuss and receive advice about potential ethical dilemmas or clarification about the above areas.

In addition to training new hires, there is a need for routine refresher training. Public service, despite cynical comment, is not static and moribund. Public service is dynamic by sheer virtue of demands made upon it. "It is a world of blurred, indistinct boundaries and situational evaluation."[27] Therefore, a one-shot, token acknowledgment of the need to act ethically in a new employee-orientation program or as a result of reaction to a string of publicized unethical acts will not deal with the organic nature of public services. Continuous attention to and carefully designed training for career employees is an ongoing need. The focus for this training should be specific and should address current problems and existing or revised statutes and regulations to deal with them. Legal decisions and administrative rulings on specific cases should be incorporated into these ongoing training efforts and disseminated widely to managers and supervisors for their information and further dissemination to their respective staffs.

The Commonwealth of Pennsylvania State Ethics Commission published the *Consolidated Rulings Digest, 1979–1987*.[28] This digest provides a condensed version of decisions rendered by the commission as a result of advisory requests or investigations that are conducted under authority of Section 7(9) of the Pennsylvania State Ethics Act, Act 170 of 1978, which became effective January 1, 1979. The act provides that public office is a public trust, and any effort to realize personal gain through public office is a violation of that trust. The 1987 *Annual Report* of the commission summarized 166 "opinions and advices" provided to heads of agencies or governmental bodies about public employee duties under the act. In the nine-year period 1979–1987 the commission issued 1,553 opinions and advices out of a total of 1,735 received. Categories of issues decided included financial interest disclosure; financial gain received; conflict of interest in association with a private corporation; use of public equipment and materials to improve private property; collecting compensation without performing services for that compensation; purchase of auto parts for private vehicles; participation in a zoning-board hearing regarding a special exception requested by an election opponent of that zoning-board member; a township supervisor voting for the retaining of a law firm that employed the supervisor's spouse; use by a mayor of his office to promote an annual mayor's ball without disclosure that the proceeds would go to the mayor's reelection fund; and more than 1,500 other examples of commission opinions and advices.

These are examples of content that should be woven into ongoing training for employees with more than one year's public service. Presentation of these and similar cases in a training environment deal with reality, reinforce behavioral standards, and provide a high degree of transfer of information and acceptable ethical practice at the workplace.

Training Support for Management-Control Systems

Another critical role that training has is to support the establishment or revision of management-control systems established to maintain the ethical practice of government. This particularly is true when the audit of management identifies unethical practices or potentially dangerous situations that need correcting. Training to support management-control systems has these characteristics:

- Installation or revision of a control system carries with it a training need that should go beyond the technical, procedural elements. For example, management-control measures to insure accountability and integrity need to look at potential ethical dilemmas that may be created by the controls. Audit-control measures need to be clarified. Audit-control and management-control separation needs to be defined. Investigation powers, safeguards, and responsibilities need to be made clear.

- Training needs are identified to meet new technologies or services. An example is the explosion of computer use by public agencies in the past decade. A full range of ethical issues have arisen. Among them are illegal use of passwords to access confidential files, manipulation of financial and audit records for personal gain, copying of copyrighted software for personal use, playing computer games during work hours, using computers for personal business, and running baseball, basketball, and football pools.

Training of managers and supervisors is particularly important because these employees have the responsibility for controlling accountability and integrity for those they supervise. The management culture will affect how the information and behaviors included in the training effort get applied at the workplace. If training is not designed to accomplish that, training outcomes will not positively affect the ethical culture of the jurisdiction concerned. Management must make certain that managers and supervisors reinforce the new information and model the behavior expected of the employees who have come through training.

AUDIT OF MANAGEMENT

The term *audit of management* encompasses the traditional concept of financial accountability as well as management accountability. Financial audits address the degree to which an agency or jurisdiction is in compliance with established policies and procedures for the allocation, disbursement, and recording of funds. Financial audits check transactions to make sure they are accurate, legal, and free of errors and illegalities. The companion to financial accountability is management accountability; together, they comprise the audit of management. The combination of these two elements represents quality control for government programs.

Each manager has responsibility for both elements as the newly appointed chief of police demonstrated. His mission was to clean up a scandal-ridden department. The mayor, who appointed him to lifetime tenure, also wanted the chief to investigate unethical and illegal practices in other city agencies. About a month after being sworn in, he was reviewing and signing purchase orders. Among them he noticed one for paint for $999.99. It looked familiar. He asked the captain responsible for department purchases if he hadn't signed a similar one a week or so ago. When told he had, the chief asked for the file on the vendors of all paint and their purchase orders for the past two years. There were about two dozen, each for $999.99. Further inquiry disclosed that city regulations required that all purchases over $1,000 be put out for competitive bids. The chief also found out that the paint vendor was a relative of the captain and that the same quality of paint could be purchased in any retail store for a lot less. The chief notified the city attorney, and legal action was brought against the captain and his relative. The captain was convicted and dismissed, losing all benefits. The vendor pleaded guilty, was fined, and was barred from dealing with any city agency in the future.

The purpose of an audit of management is to identify operational errors or problems, uncover discrepancies in records, and confirm those systems that are working well. The management team assigned to carry out the audit of management provides an independent check on management. The team audit can identify potential problems when they are most amenable to solution and can prevent more serious problems.

An effective audit of management has these characteristics:[29]

- Scheduled review of financial record keeping and accounting, including compliance with the law in keeping separate funds separate, making expenditures within approved procedures, compliance with generally accepted accounting principles, and solicitation of recommendations for improvement from staff responsible for these task areas.

- Verification that monies received are accounted for and properly managed, including unannounced spot checks made at random to verify that cash on hand matches receipts.

- Review of pay scales to make sure employees are being paid according to proper pay scales, and periodic comparisons of pay scales with other, similar jurisdictions and the private sector.

- Verification that everyone on the payroll is, in fact, working or otherwise accounted for and documentation of all personnel actions for completeness and currency.

- Check of actual time worked with payroll records and spot checks to verify that work time is being used for public service.

- Review of benefits program for correct use and recording. For example, are there patterns of "Friday-Monday" absences that may indicate abuse?

- Scheduled and random inventory checks to make sure things are where they should be and that consumable supplies conform to inventory and use records.

- Review of computer use and passwords for confidential files to insure maintenance of confidentiality, private use, and phantom invoicing and check requisitions. Attention also should be focused on use of computers for baseball and football pools, casting horoscopes, and similar improprieties. The threat of "hackers" infecting computer systems also needs to be addressed. Robert Morris, the Cornell hacker, whose virus program clogged thousands of computers in 1988, may not have intended serious consequences with his electronic sabotage. However, to deceive others, invade their property, cause significant loss of time and money, and disrupt the activity of others clearly is unethical.

- Review of the efficiency and effectiveness of units with input measures (allocation, staff, equipment, time) and performance measures (numbers of transactions and their quality, handling of complaints, and the time it takes to resolve them). For example, federal agencies estimated that in FYs 1980 through 1985, it took an average of 482 days from the date a formal complaint of sexual harassment was filed until the date the complaint was resolved.[30] The question managers should ask about this average is whether or not it is appropriate and, if not, what needs to be done to improve the time for this administrative process.

• Review of the proper use of "perks" such as official cars, travel funds, expense accounts, memberships, or other privileges related to specific jobs or assignments.

• Check of performance appraisals to determine if ethical issues that focus on specific areas of vulnerability for that agency are reviewed.

INVESTIGATION

Audit of management may not identify all instances of financial or managerial unethical practice, let alone inefficiencies or poor-quality performance in service delivery. Audit of management cannot anticipate specific complaints or charges brought against individuals or agency units alleging unethical or illegal practices. When such allegations are made, it may be necessary to appoint a unit to investigate the matter. It makes no difference whether or not the allegations originate inside or outside the organization. The matter must be followed up to determine its validity. Management must assume that it is implicated and involved even if it is convinced that it isn't. Management must accept the responsibility for unethical practices of employees that it supervises. By commission or omission, management is responsible. Therefore, management must set up either a temporary or permanent group to investigate complaints or charges and determine whether or not there appears to be enough basis in fact to pursue the matter further. If it is determined that further investigation is warranted, appropriate representatives from management, law enforcement, and legal departments of the jurisdiction should be convened, briefed on the allegations, and asked to prepare a plan to pursue the matter further. A decision also should be made about bringing in an outside expert in those situations in which technology or other special knowledge is needed. The independence of the investigative unit is essential to insure its integrity and public perception of the truthfulness and impartiality of its findings. Legislation establishing the special prosecutor in the federal government came about because of public dissatisfaction about alleged and proven unethical and illegal practices of executive branch appointees.

The investigative unit should have carte blanche access to records, audits, and employees. In the initial stages of the process it is important to insure that nobody's constitutional rights are violated and that those being asked to provide information are clear that they have the right to answer or not answer any or all questions. The purpose of this preliminary inquiry is to determine whether formal proceedings are necessary.

To the degree possible, the results should be made a matter of public record and available to the public. The investigative team, however, must be sensitive to those situations in which public disclosure of ongoing investigations might result in possible harm to witnesses or employees against whom formal charges might be brought. The unit also must consider that premature disclosure of certain information might lead to destruction of evidence by employees under investigation. This first-level inquiry into complaints and charges is fraught with booby traps. It requires great care and sensitivity to protect all concerned and arrive at a decision to proceed or not with a formal complaint by the prosecutor's office.

Management has an inherent responsibility to be open about unethical practices that surface in its jurisdiction. Recent history demonstrates over and over again that denial and attempts to "stonewall" unethical practices may delay their illumination. But sooner or later, they come to light. When management circles the wagons, keeps the blinds drawn, attempts to keep the public in the dark, and hides its dirty laundry in the closet, unethical practices grow and flourish like some photophobic mold. When management is proactive in identifying and exposing unethical practices, when the public perception is the management cares and is doing something about it, the environment becomes hostile to these practices, and the culture changes radically for the better. When leaders lead ethically, followers follow ethically.

In one jurisdiction, a police captain met with officers in his precinct at break time to discuss some new patrol strategies. When the meeting ended, the captain went to pay for his coffee and danish. The cashier said the management never accepted money from "their friends in blue." The captain paid. When he returned to the precinct he sent a memorandum to his precinct staff reminding them of the city policy prohibiting anyone from accepting any free gifts, including food. He stressed the provisions for disciplinary action should anyone violate the policy. A few days later one of the officers told the captain he was glad the captain did what he did. The officer said that the restrooms in this restaurant were filthy, but he felt funny about reporting this to the health department because of the free coffee and danish. He said he now would do what was right and report the violation.

The preliminary investigation exhibits these characteristics, in this sequence:[31]

- The complaint is received and reviewed by the appropriate agency staff. The complaint is matched against immediately available evidence—payroll, audit, purchase vouchers, inventory check, mileage records, petty cash receipts and cash on hand, cancelled checks, travel receipts, or other records. The person with the complaint may be interviewed to further define the nature of and support for it.

- A preliminary decision about the charge or complaint is made. If it appears groundless, it is dropped. If it appears as if further investigation is proper and warranted, the team is authorized to proceed further within proper legal boundaries.

- A plan is developed that defines what evidence is needed to prove or disprove the complaint or charge. A log is started and decisions recorded.

- The necessary employees are contacted, the nature of the complaint or charge explained, the purpose clarified to identify or disprove unethical practice, and the information collected and entered in the log.

- The investigation is continued to the point that it is possible to determine whether the allegation is valid.

- The investigation team determines the action needed. If the results do not support the allegation, management is advised on a response to the person making the complaint or charge and the person(s) against whom the allegations were made.

When it is clear that there is public knowledge about the charges and that the charges involve one or more people, management should be swift in making known that the charges are without credence. If the investigative team reports that the charge or complaint is verified and an illegal act has been committed, the matter should be turned over to the criminal justice system for prosecution. When the act does not constitute a crime but is improper or unethical behavior, the matter should be referred to the manager concerned for disciplinary action and, when appropriate, modification in policy and procedure.

MANAGEMENT CONTROL

Consider a jurisdiction where each employee decides and controls what he would like to do and how to do it. Add to that empowering the employee with the authority for monitoring and evaluating personal performance. The formula adds up to chaos or worse. The purpose of putting management controls in place is to insure that the practice of government is conducted efficiently, effectively, and ethically. Management control defines and monitors what employees do, desired levels of performance and their measurements, and appropriate feedback. Management control should be broadly based and not narrowly focused on preventing and disclosing unethical practices. Management needs to focus on the broader aspects of employee performance within agency operational guidelines. If this is done properly, unethical practices will be identified and dealt with appropriately.

It makes more sense to establish required reporting, disclosure, and evaluation procedures that can identify and correct improprieties than to try to prevent every conceivable one. A management culture that promotes ethical practices and encourages discretion in decision making will avoid stopping or delaying activities or making them more costly, inefficient, and ineffective. Too much control can have the same effect as too little.

The Building Department processed plans very slowly; the department head knew there were some severe inefficiencies, but was spending most of his time trying to get the job of building inspector upgraded and a test of competence built into the hiring procedure. He was horrified to find that the inefficiency had resulted in developers—who had to pay extra interest on construction loans for every day of delay—paying bribes to get important, expensive jobs through the department with a minimum of delay.

As a result, he overhauled procedures in the entire department, introduced several new forms that had to be filled out to indicate who was working on every permit application every day, requiring verification by a supervisor, and accounting for time down to 10-minute intervals. The forms were unwieldy, time-consuming, and unrealistic; the result was that under the new procedures, the Building Department processed plans even more slowly. He was again horrified to find that developers were still paying bribes to get important, expensive jobs through the department with a minimum of delay.[32]

Increasing controls with the intent of reducing unethical practices may have the countereffect, as the Building Department head discovered. Excessive controls may make it more "efficient" for contractors to bribe government officials to expedite their decisions. If contractors know that decisions are being made within realistic time frames and that bribes will have no effect on the decision-making process, there is no incentive for this unethical practice. In this scenario, the contractor also will know that the offer or payment of a bribe will lead to prosecution.

An effective management-control system considers not only what work is expected to be done but how employee performance matches these expectations. An effective management-control system should reflect detailed knowledge of the activities to be controlled. The system also should involve participation by those for whom performance expectations are set. In putting a management-control system in place, consideration should be given to:[33]

1. Looking at existing system operations from the perspective of the public to be served to identify inefficiencies. Examples: street crews waiting for materials trucks and heavy equipment to arrive, equipment ordered and installed and no plans for training its users, mul-

tiple signatures needed on routine documents with persons authorized to sign in multiple locations, another form created to "solve" a problem.

2. Looking at similar systems and practices in other jurisdictions that might be adopted/adapted to improve performance or reduce opportunities and incentives for unethical acts. Examples: policies against accepting any gifts of any value, improved management of criminal investigations based on solvability factors, appointing and training ethics counselors in each government department as primary resources for employees with ethical problems or issues, establishing an ombudsman as an independent resource to protect employee rights as they relate to reporting alleged unethical practices.

3. Practicing participative management by involving employees (the system "users") who will be impacted by the decision on performance standards. Example: forming quality circles in motor-vehicle maintenance shops, forming task groups for review and recommendations concerning a new word processing system, creating barrier analysis and removal employee-involvement teams (BARE-IT).

4. Developing practical and realistic standards and expectations for getting the work done. Examples: patrol car assignments based on crime analysis reports, building inspectors performing x site inspections a week and rotating on a biweekly basis to different areas, production typists averaging y pages of correct copy an hour, all purchases over $z let out for sealed competitive bids and public bid openings.

5. Budgeting should reflect expected work load in relation to numbers of employees needed to do the work. Examples: nursing staffing patterns to reflect average census by in-patient units and shifts, overtime resources for street repair and maintenance crews during seasons of inclement weather.

6. Determining and requiring the least number of reports to verify if the work did, in fact, get done as expected and who did or did not do it and making sure the manager who supervises the manager responsible for the work gets a copy of the report.

7. Monitoring reports and spot checking performance to validate that the system works. Example: a supervisor was pleased at the performance of an employee who served as an "in-house consultant" to other departments in this jurisdiction. The employee's reports were detailed and cited considerable success in helping these other departments solve their problems. The supervisor needed to reach

this employee out on assignment. He called the person listed as being visited on that day by his employee and asked to speak to the employee. The person never heard of the employee. When confronted, the employee admitted that half of the time he made up the reports and usually took the time off to take care of personal business.

8. Developing a performance appraisal process based on the above criteria that identifies deficiencies and plans to resolve them, as well as performance that meets or exceeds expectations.

NOTES

1. Bill Boyarsky and Nancy Boyarsky, *Backroom Politics* (Los Angeles: J. P. Tarcher, Inc., 1974): 2.

2. David A. Stockman, *The Triumph of Politics: Why the Reagan Revolution Failed* (New York: Harper and Row, 1986): 124.

3. William Greider, "The Education of David Stockman," *The Atlantic Monthly*, December 1981, p. 39.

4. Paul Blustein, "Did Darman Outsmart Himself on the Budget?" *Washington Post*, February 26, 1989, p. C2.

5. Ibid.

6. *Practical Ethics for Chiefs of Missions and All Department of State and Foreign Service Employees* (Washington, D.C.: U.S. Department of State, Office of the Inspector General, August, 1986): ii.

7. Ibid., 1–21.

8. Leslie Maitland Werner, "Investigating Wedtech, Mr. Meese's Ethics Are Once Again Scrutinized," *New York Times*, May 17, 1987, p. E5.

9. Michael E. Shaheen, Counsel, U.S. Department of Justice, Office of Professional Responsibility, "Results of Our Review of the Independent Counsel's Inquiry Into Certain Activities of Attorney General Edwin Meese III," Memorandum to Dick Thornburgh, Attorney General, October 28, 1988, pp. 60–61.

10. Ibid., p. 61.

11. "More on Mr. Meese," *New York Times*, July 28, 1988, p. A20.

12. Counsel for Attorney General Edwin Meese III, "Response to the Report of the Office of Professional Responsibility," January 16, 1989, p. 16, in *Ethics and Government Reporter*.

13. U.S. General Accounting Office, *Reagan-Bush Transition Team Activities in Six Selected Agencies* (Washington, D.C.: U.S. General Accounting Office, February 26, 1982): 51.

14. Mark T. Lilla, "Ethos, 'Ethics,' and Public Service," *The Public Interest*, no. 63 (Spring 1981): 16.

15. Adapted from T. R. Lyman, T. W. Fletcher, and J. A. Gardiner, *Prevention, Detection and Correction of Corruption in Local Government: A Presentation of Potential Models* (Washington, D.C.: U.S. Department of Justice, Law Enforcement Assistance Administration, July 1978): 32.

16. Adapted from David T. Austern, et al., *Maintaining Municipal Integrity, Trainer's Handbook* (Washington, D.C.: U.S. Department of Justice, Law Enforcement Assistance Administration, 1978): 77.

17. Mark Shields, "He Was Just Pleasing Nancy, So No Big Deal," *Washington Post*, January 28, 1989, p. A21.

18. Ibid.

19. Richard Cohen, "Nancy's Own Little Scandal, A Million-Dollar Deception Is Not Trivial," *Washington Post*, October 23, 1988, p. C5.

20. "Index on Clippings of Alleged Violations and Other Improprieties by Reagan Administration Appointees," House Subcommittee on Civil Service, October 4, 1988, 28 pp.

21. Subcommittee on Human Resources, Committee on Post Office and Civil Service, House of Representatives. Hearing on "Reauthorization of the Office of Government Ethics," March 31, 1988, p. 42.

22. Executive Order 1122, 1978.

23. National Aeronautics and Space Administration, *Standards of Conduct for NASA Employees* (Washington, D.C.: National Aeronautics and Space Administration, 1987): 5–1.

24. Ibid., p. 6–1.

25. Carol W. Lewis, *Scruples and Scandals: A Handbook on Public Ethics for State and Local Government Officials and Employees in Connecticut* (Storrs, CT: The Institute of Public Service and The Institute of Urban Research, The University of Connecticut, 1986), 27.

26. Austern, *Maintaining Municipal Integrity*, 133–35.

27. Lewis, *Scruples and Scandals*, 1.

28. Commonwealth of Pennsylvania State Ethics Commission, *Consolidated Rulings Digest* (Harrisburg, PA: Commonwealth of Pennsylvania State Ethics Commission, 1988): 139 pp.

29. Austern, *Maintaining Municipal Integrity*, 130–31.

30. U.S. Merit Systems Protection Board, *Sexual Harassment in the Federal Government: An Update*, June 1988, p. 31.

31. Austern, *Maintaining Municipal Integrity*, 136–38.

32. Ibid., 127.

33. Ibid., 128.

Appendix A

Ethical Dilemmas Score Sheet

HOW TO SCORE YOUR ANSWERS

The table below has a score for each yes or no question. Check to see if you received a 1, 2, or 3 for each question. Then add up your score and consult the "What Each Score Means" explanation that follows the table.

Question No.	1	2	3	4	5	6	7
Yes Score	2	1	1	1	2	1	1
No Score	1	2	2	3	1	3	3

Question No.	8	9	10	11	12	13	14
Yes Score	1	1	2	1	2	1	1
No Score	2	2	1	3	1	3	2

WHAT EACH SCORE MEANS

A score of 1 for an answer shows that you have high ethical standards, are clearly a dedicated elected or appointed official, and set a good example for those around you. You may have had strong laws or codes of ethics in your community that have helped you define standards and expectations. If you scored a total of 14–18, good for you!

A score of 2 for an answer means that although you may not "break the law" or delegate others to do so, neither do you assertively pursue wrongdoing or "marginal" practices. Probably, you are more interested in keeping things running smoothly than in righting wrong. If you scored 19–24, you need to do some serious reflection on your own vulnerability to unethical practices.

A score of 3 for an answer shows trouble. This score indicates a tendency toward conduct that is based on no ethics or values or shows a disregard for any perspective reflecting an ethical commitment. If you scored 25 or higher, hire a good lawyer.

Further Reading

Baker, Ross K. *The New Fat Cats: Members of Congress as Political Bene-factors*. Priority Press Publications, 1989.

Formation of political action committees by members of Congress to raise money for campaigns of congressional colleagues, potential negative impact on the political process.

Bernstein, Carl, and Woodward, Bob. *All the President's Men*. Simon and Shuster, 1974.

A classic in investigative journalism that highlights the important role of the press in protecting the public from unethical and corrupt politicians. This book follows in the best "muckraking" traditions of earlier in this century, and underlines the need for eternal vigilance in monitoring all branches of our government.

Bowman, James S., and Elliston, Frederick. *Ethics, Government, and Public Policy: A Reference Guide*. Greenwood Press, 1988.

Contents are grouped under the headings analytical approaches; ethical dilemmas and standards for public servants; techniques and methods in ethical policy-making; and, studies of systemic issues in government.

Boyarsky, William, and Boyarsky, Nancy. *Backroom Politics*. Tarcher, 1974.

Deal-making, secret trades, the give-and-take of campaign contributions, and the desire to stay in power are documented in this look at the inner workings of the political machinery and those who operate it. Specific techniques successfully used to attack entrenched political systems by aroused citizen groups all over the country are detailed.

Conable, Alfred. *Tigers of Tammany*. Holt, Rhinehart and Winston, 1967.
Historical development of the notorious political machine made famous by Thomas Nast's newspaper cartoons. Traces the founding and perfection of the "spoils system" and some of Tammany's more famous Sachems, including Bosses Tweed and Plunkitt. The impact of Tammany Hall on national presidential elections as far back as Thomas Jefferson's time is described.

Denhardt, Kathryn G. *The Ethics of Public Services: Resolving Moral Dilemmas in Public Organizations*. Greenwood Press, 1988.
Contents include public administration ethics, the social, historical and organizational context of public administration, paths to a more ethical public administration for the individual and the organization, and an application of ethics in practice.

Donahue, Ann Marie, ed. *Ethics in Politics and Government*. H. W. Wilson and Co., 1989.
Compendium of articles, congressional reports, and other related documents organized into four major sections: Moral Principle and Foreign Policy; Ethics and the Executive Branch; Integrity and Compromise in Congress; and, Character, Moral Judgement, and Ethical Leadership.

Drew, Elizabeth. *Politics and Money: The New Road to Corruption*. Macmillan, 1983.
Describes how big money flows from organized interests and influences congressional behavior, and how private money plays a major role in presidential politics. Discusses the extent to which members of Congress are preoccupied with the omnipresent need to raise campaign funds and how organized interests collect money for, and get the most out of support for, selected candidates.

Henriques, Diana B. *The Machinery of Greed: Public Authority Abuse and What to Do about It*. Lexington Books, 1986.
Instances of alleged mismanagement, bribery, political influence peddling, and other questionable practices with some suggestions for prevention.

Jaworski, Leon. *The Right and the Power: The Prosecution of Watergate*. Reader's Digest Press, 1976.
Legal and strategic behind-the-scenes maneuvering between the Watergate special prosecutor and the men who served President Nixon and tried to cover his involvement and support for

the Watergate break-in and other "dirty tricks." An excellent chronical of the refusal of a former prosecutor at the Nuremburg War Crimes trials to ignore the rights of society and the ethical practice of government.

Riordan, William. *Plunkitt of Tammany Hall: A Series of Very Plain Talks on Very Practical Politics*. E. P. Dutton, 1963.

Unusually candid series of interviews with the Tammany Hall Sachem who immortalized the difference between "honest graft" and "dishonest graft." A good look at the way local politics, through the "Boss" system, operated to turn shanty-town paupers into uptown millionaires.

Roberts, Robert N. *White House Ethics: The History of the Politics of Conflict of Interest Regulations*. Greenwood Press, 1988.

Development and implementation of standards of conduct regulations for employees and officials of the executive branch, beginning with the Truman presidency.

Steinberg, Alfred. *Bosses*. Macmillan, 1972.

A look at the major political machines operating in America in the first half of this century. Detailed descriptions of bosses who ran roughshod over Jersey City, Memphis, Boston, New York City, Louisiana, and Georgia, and the strategies they invented and employed to maintain power, control jobs, and line their bank accounts illuminate and define the "Corrupter" ethic.

Weinberg, Arthur, and Weinberg, Lila. *The Muckrakers: The Era in Journalism that Moved America to Reform*. Simon and Shuster, 1961.

A recreation of an era in American history through the efforts of the original "angry young men and women" writers of the twentieth century. Their efforts gave the Progressive political movement the impetus in achieving needed social and political legislation in housing, prison reform, pure food and drug laws, life insurance regulation, and improvements in the conduct of federal, state and local government.

Woodward, Bob, and Bernstein, Carl. *The Final Days*. Simon and Shuster, 1976.

The rest of the Watergate story, detailing the desperate measures to save the Nixon presidency, and the disarray, jealousies and rivalries attendant to the resignation of the President.

Index